Georgia Land Lottery Research

Georgia
Land Lottery
Research

Paul K. Graham

Georgia Land Lottery Research

Address inquiries to:
Georgia Genealogical Society
P.O. Box 550247
Atlanta, GA 30355-2747
www.gagensociety.org

Printed in the United States of America

Library of Congress Control Number: 2010916210

Hardcover ISBN-13: 978-0-9789916-1-6
ISBN-10: 0-9789916-1-3

To the staff of the Georgia Archives—
past, present, and future.

Contents

Illustrations

Maps

Preface

Georgia distributed three quarters of its public lands by lottery. The associated records are important for genealogists and historians who wish to document the land and the people who participated in these events. The grid survey system makes it easy to find land lottery lots today, and land lot numbers are included in legal descriptions of property from the grant to today. Land lot grants and plats form the first record of individual ownership of each tract of land in the lottery areas. This book is designed for researchers who wish to develop a foundational understanding of the land lottery survey system, the lottery process, and the records that provide documentation of this part of Georgia history.

The book is a guide to researching the land lotteries on site at the Georgia Archives. After an introduction to the land lottery process and survey system, it includes a chapter outlining strategies for the most common research goals. Each research strategy leads to other chapters that explain major elements of the process in detail. The later chapters explain records of participants, fortunate drawers, grants, and plats. Following the fundamentals, a final narrative chapter speaks to the variety of additional records that are important for land lottery research but do not apply to every lot. The final section of the book is organized by land lottery and includes key facts, maps, and records for each original land lottery county. Physical locations identified in this book (microfilm, volume, and box numbers) are used to locate records at the archives and are subject to change.

The book was produced in part to fulfill one requirement of the Master of Heritage Preservation degree at Georgia State University. All proceeds from its sale go to the Georgia Genealogical Society. Unless specified, document images are courtesy of the Georgia Archives and used with permission.

The Land Lotteries

Georgia held eight land lotteries from 1805 to 1833. The events are historically unique and related records are important to historians and genealogists performing research in Georgia. Although land lotteries were used before and after, Georgia's remain the largest both in land area and number of participants.

Headright Land System

Until 1805, Georgia distributed its land through the headright land system. Land was available to individuals based on the number of heads in their household. Men were eligible for 200 acres in their own right, plus an additional 50 acres for each dependant, up to 1,000 acres total. The eastern and coastal counties of Georgia make up the headright area of the state (see Map 1).

Three problems plagued the headright system as it was implemented in Georgia. First, irregular plot shapes resulted from the use of the metes and bounds survey system, causing confusion among land owners and leading to numerous boundary disputes and other lawsuits (see Figure 1). Second, the process placed a financial burden on participants, involving short-term expenses related to travel, surveying, court fees, and grant fees, along with the long-term expenses related to maintenance of survey lines. Third, the structure of county land courts invited corruption, allowing well-connected individuals to obtain grants to many more acres of land than was allowed by law.

Land Frauds

Two significant land frauds rocked Georgia in the 1790s. The Pine Barrens Speculation involved fraudulent granting of land in the area in and around Montgomery County. The Yazoo Land Fraud involved the sale of Georgia's western lands in present-day Mississippi to land speculators in return for bribes to government officials. When Georgia changed to a new land distribution system in 1803, it did so in response to the land frauds and problems inherent to the headright system.

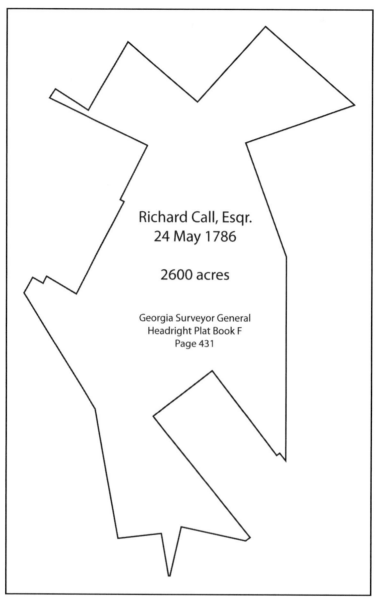

Figure 1. Diagram of thirty-sided plat made to Richard Call.

Georgia ceded its western lands to the United States in 1802, being everything west of the current boundary with Alabama, stretching to the Mississippi River. The same year, the Creek Indians ceded two tracts of land in Georgia to the United States. One strip lay along the western bank of the Oconee River. The other lay between the Saint Mary's River and Altamaha River on the western boundaries of Glynn and Camden counties. In 1805, this became the first land surveyed and distributed under the new lottery system. Seven more land lotteries would follow, finally concluding in 1833. Anyone interested in learning more about the history of each land lottery should read Farris Cadle's *Georgia Land Surveying History and Law*, a well-written and accessible history.

New Land System

The structure of the Georgia land lotteries is based on the two fundamental parts of every land system: the **survey system** and the **disposition process**. In response to the inherent problems of the metes and bounds survey system, Georgia established a new survey system made up of uniformly sized squares, mimicking the Public Land Survey System of townships, ranges, and sections taking shape in the Midwest states. Rather than the section, the base survey unit in Georgia is called a **Land Lot**. A few hundred land lots make up each **Land District**, and multiple land districts make up an **Original County**. For the most part, the three units form the foundation of legal descriptions of land in the land lottery areas of Georgia. The exception to the rule is the Cherokee Territory, which was created as one county with four numbered sections. In original Cherokee County, section numbers are an additional element of land lot legal descriptions.

Coincident with the development of a new survey system, the Georgia General Assembly adopted a dramatically different land disposition process—random chance. Lotteries with money prizes were widely used at the time to fund charitable organizations and public works projects, so legislators did not have to look far for inspiration. Eligible participants registered in their county of residence during a proscribed period of time; the names were then sent to the state where lottery commissioners wrote them on tickets to be placed in a large drum. Only in the 1805 lottery was this procedure not followed. That year, names were read from four books. In addition to the names, tickets containing lot—or "prize"—numbers were placed in a separate drum. Although the exact procedure changed from lottery to lottery as the commissioners gained experience, each involved the random assignment of names to lots. When a participant's name matched to a land lot, that person was given first right to obtain a grant to the land. However, winning in a land lottery did not guarantee that a grant would be issued to that person.

Georgia's land lottery land system eliminated most of the problems inherent in the headright land system. It used uniform surveys, involved a transparent and accountable process, and allowed more social and economic classes to participate in the land grant process.

Land Lottery Process

Treaty
    Before Georgia distributed land to citizens, it obtained title to the land through treaties made between the United States and either Creek or Cherokee Indians.

Law
    Once in control of the land, the legislature approved a law outlining the process whereby the land would be distributed, including surveys, registration, grants, drawing, and other concerns.

Surveys
    Using the land lottery law as a guide, surveyors chosen by the legislature marked the various survey lines, including original county boundaries, land district lines, and land lots.

Registration
    For a period of time following publication of each land lottery law, eligible citizens went to their local justice court or courthouse to register. Participants were called "persons entitled to draws."

Drawing
    After registering eligible participants and surveying land lots, the land lottery was held. Those whose name was drawn against a land lot had first right to the land. People who won land lots were called "fortunate drawers."

Grants
    Grants represent the transfer of land ownership from the state to an individual. Fortunate drawers who chose to act on a winning draw obtained a grant to their land lot. Others purchased fractional or reverted lots.

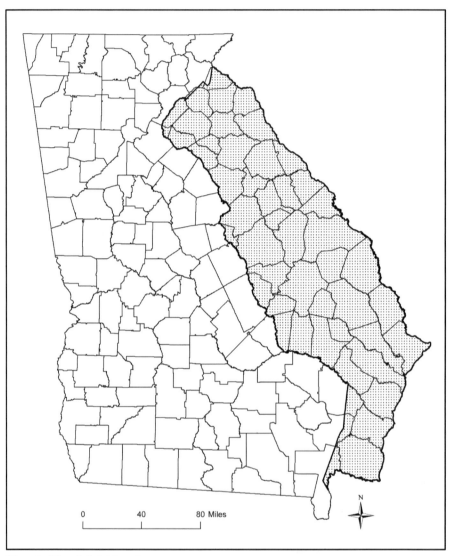

Map 1. Headright land.

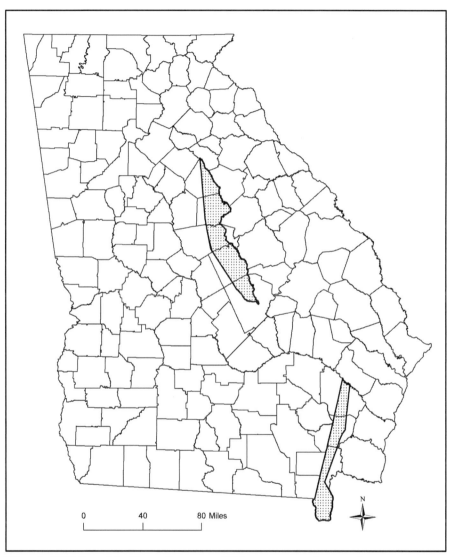

Map 2. 1805 Land Lottery. See page 77 for maps and records.

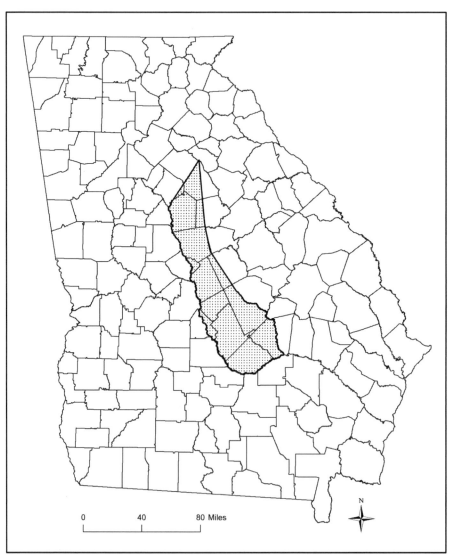

Map 3. 1807 Land Lottery. See page 85 for maps and records.

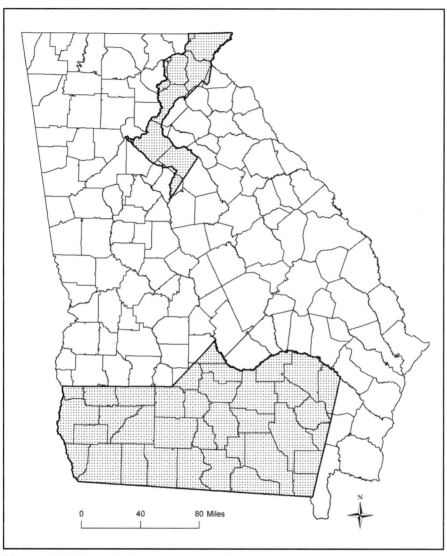

Map 4. 1820 Land Lottery. See page 91 for maps and records.

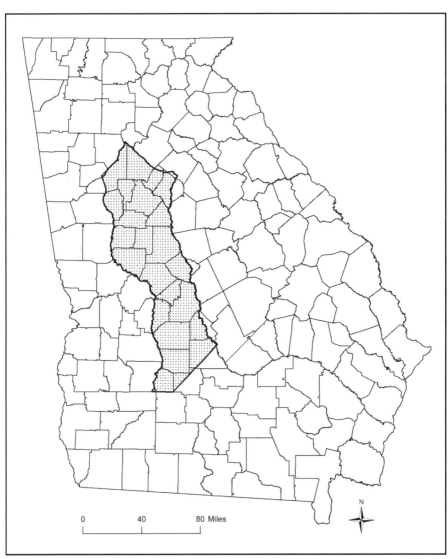

0   40   80 Miles

N

Map 5. 1821 Land Lottery. See page 111 for maps and records.

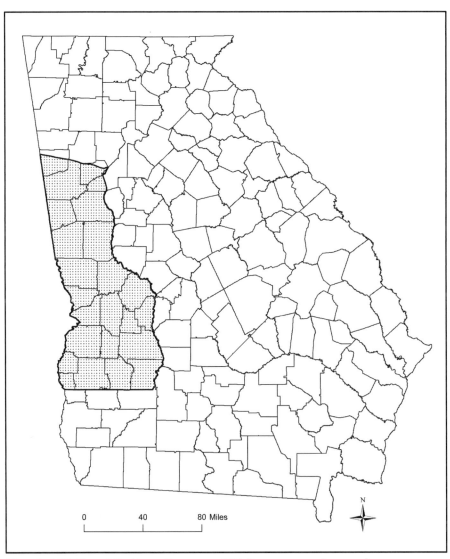

Map 6. 1827 Land Lottery. See page 123 for maps and records.

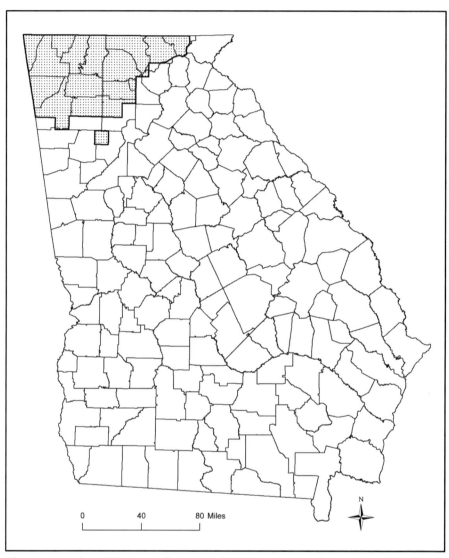

Map 7. 1832 Land Lottery. See page 137 for maps and records.

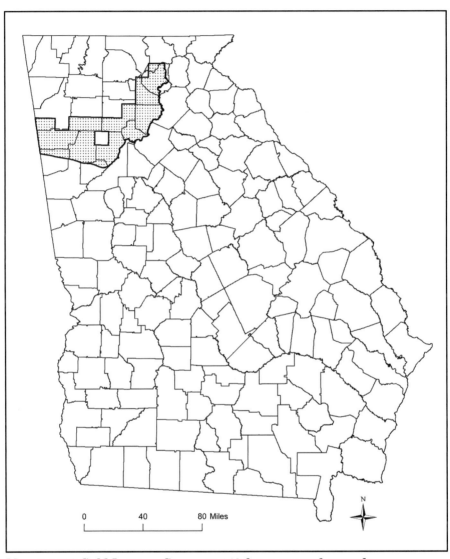

Map 8. 1832 Gold Lottery. See page 149 for maps and records.

Land lots are the foundational survey unit in the land lottery areas of Georgia, similar to the Federal *section*. They are square, except those that lie along irregular boundaries such as rivers. Their size and orientation vary between land lottery areas. See the land lottery chapters (beginning on page 77) for lot size and orientation information for each original county. As the survey unit for state land grants, land lots continue to be used in legal descriptions. The regular shape and numbering of land lots allows researchers to identify specific tracts of land, exemplified by Figure 2, showing an 1870 land lot map of the area in and around the city of Atlanta in Fulton County.

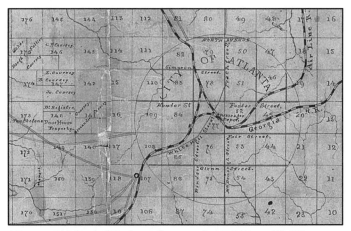

Figure 2. *Map of Fulton County*, by William Phillips

Survey Organization

Land lottery surveys are laid out on four levels of organization. Original Cherokee County includes a fifth level. These are the land lottery, original county, section (in Cherokee only), district, and land lot. They were surveyed in stages. First, the treaty boundary was marked. Using the description of the land lottery area provided by law, a surveyor then marked off the boundaries of each original county. Following him, other surveyors marked the boundaries of districts, ultimately finishing with the district surveyors—the men who surveyed each land lot.

Land Lottery

The first level of survey is the total area distributed in a single land lottery. Boundaries of each land lottery area are defined by language in treaties and state law. Most treaty boundaries are defined by major waterways, old trails, and straight lines with no connection to existing features. In some cases, like the 1820 lottery, the land lottery area is made up of multiple treaty areas. Map 9 shows the total area distributed through the 1821 land lottery process.

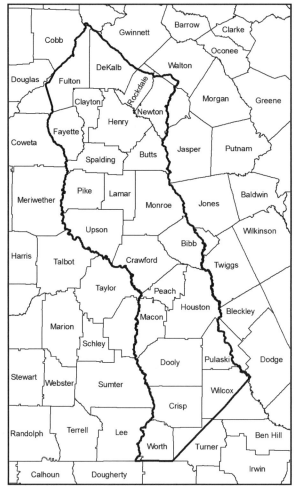

Map 9. 1821 Land Lottery Area

Original County

The second level of land lottery survey is the original county. Except for the 1832 lotteries, each land lottery area contains multiple original counties. These large areas of territory make up the first part of any land lot legal description. Map 10 shows the 1821 land lottery area and its five original counties: Fayette, Henry, Monroe, Houston, and Dooly. Original Houston County is highlighted. It is not necessary to identify the lottery when describing land; by specifying the original county, the lottery year is implied.

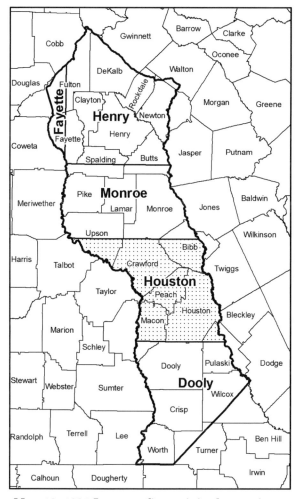

Map 10. 1821 Lottery, five original counties

Section

Sections are used in original Cherokee County, which contains four numbered sections. When describing land in original Cherokee County, section numbers must be used along with the county, district, and land lot. See pages 138 through 156 for Cherokee County section maps.

Land District

Original counties are divided into districts, each containing tens of thousands of acres of land. Land districts are numbered sequentially within each county. Map 11 shows original Houston County with its sixteen land districts. Gray areas are reserves, held out from the land lottery (see pages 72–74). District 13 is highlighted. Map 12 (opposite) shows Houston County, District 13, and its land lots. The town of Perry, Georgia, lies just north of original Houston County, District 13, in original Houston County, District 10. Interstate 75 runs through the district's west side.

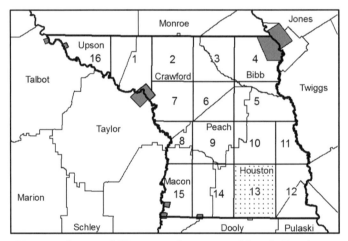

Map 11. Original Houston County and land districts

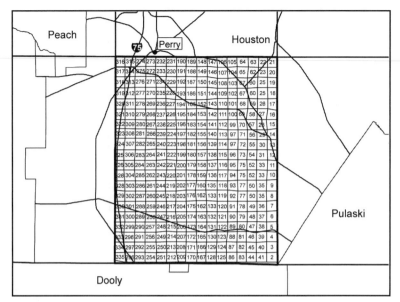

Map 12. Houston County, District 13, and land lots

Land Lot

Land lots are the smallest original survey unit in the land lottery areas of Georgia and are numbered sequentially within each land district. Some land lots were given letter designations (A, B, etc.) because the surveyor initially forgot to give them a number. Land lots range in size from 40 acres to 490 acres, depending on the land lottery and their location. See the land lottery chapters for details. Map 13 (next page) shows Land Lot 313 in District 13, original Houston County. Today, the land lot contains part of the Georgia National Fairgrounds and Agricenter. As is clear from the map, the lot is not perfectly square. Difficult surveying conditions and inaccurate instruments resulted in many land lots being surveyed as rectangles and parallelograms.

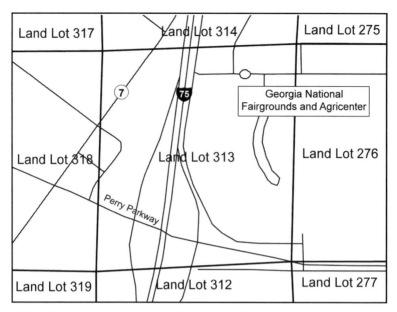

Map 13. Houston County, District 13, Land Lot 313

The majority of surveyed lots in the land lotteries are "whole" lots. Whole lots are defined by law as square lots and large fractions (as specified). The following plat for land in original Houston County shows a 202 ½ acre land lot on the waters of Indian Creek. It was surveyed 17 August 1821 by John T. Forth, District Surveyor.

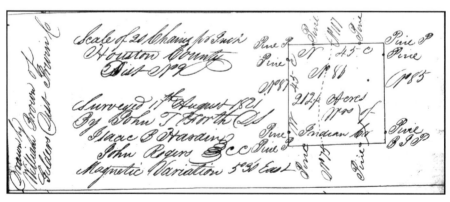

Figure 3. Land lot plat, Houston County, District 9, Land lot 86

"Fractions" or "fractional lots" are surveyed lots of irregular shape and less than a size prescribed by law. Most fractions result from surveys along rivers. Through 1827, fractions were not drawn in the lotteries; instead, they were held out and sold at auction. Fractional lots in the Cherokee Territory were drawn in the final land lottery in 1833. The following plat for land in original Wayne County shows a fractional survey along the Altamaha River. It was surveyed 20 March 1805 by Abner Davis, District Surveyor.

Figure 4. Land lot plat, Wayne County, District 3, Land Lot 163

Figure 5. Land lots near Eastman visible from the air.

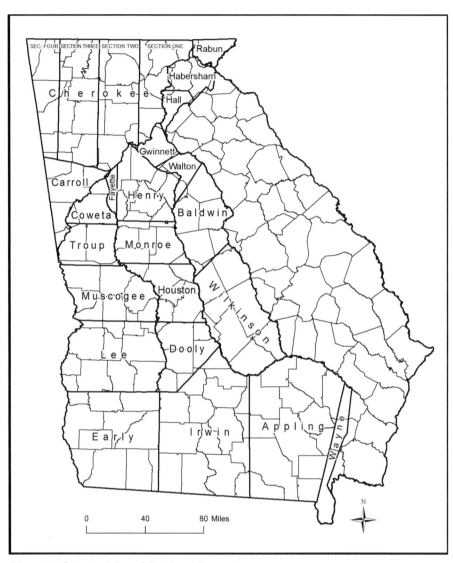

Map 14. Original Land Lottery Counties.

Describing Land Lottery Land

Land lot descriptions are formed using the county name, district number, and land lot number. In areas of original Cherokee, the section number is used. The order of information varies depending on the person writing the description. For instance, both legal descriptions below are written with the district first, then county, then land lot number. It is also appropriate to write the information with the land lot first, then district, then county, or reversed with the county first and land lot last. Historically, the "district, county, lot" order is common, and modern legal descriptions are written in "lot, district, county" order.

1820 Georgia Land Lottery

In Figure 6, the description of land in District 9, Colquitt County [original Irwin County], reads "...all that tract or lot of Land situate lying and being in the ninth District of Colquitt County Known and distinguished in the plan of said District as lot No 16 sixteen said to contain 490 acres more or less...."

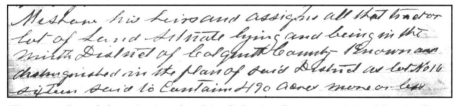

Figure 6. Legal description, land in Colquitt County, original Irwin Co.

1832 Georgia Gold Lottery

In Figure 7, the description of land in District 9, Section 3, original Cherokee County, reads "...all that tract or parcel of land situate, lying & being in the ninth District of the third section Cherokee County, Known & distinguished in the plan of said District as lot number Three (3) containing one hundred & sixty (160) acres more or less...."

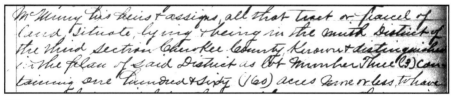

Figure 7. Legal description, land in original Cherokee County

Land Lot Descriptions Today

While boundary lines of land lots may be revised over time, land lots themselves do not move and are not renumbered. Using the land lot, district, and county, current owners of land can trace the title history of their property to the grant. For example, certain land was surveyed in 1821 as Land Lot 207, District 14, in original Henry County, and covered an area of 202½ acres. Today, the land lot is part of Fulton County, which was created in December 1853. The Collier Heights residential subdivision sits in part of the land lot. This legal description of a Collier Heights subdivision lot demonstrates the use of the land lot, district, and county in a deed from 2008.

> ALL THAT TRACT OR PARCEL OF LAND LYING AND BEING IN LAND LOT 207 OF THE 14TH DISTRICT OF FULTON COUNTY, GEORGIA, BEING LOT 7, BLOCK A, COLLIER HEIGHTS SUBDIVISION, AS PER PLAT THEREOF RECORDED IN PLAT BOOK 30, PAGE 34, FULTON COUNTY RECORDS.

Why District Numbers are Important

The necessity of complete legal descriptions, with lot number, district, and county, is made clear by this anecdote from the 1827 land lottery published in the *Macon Telegraph* (4 June 1827, p. 2).

"The tract of land supposed to be the most valuable in the new Territory remained in the wheel until the day's drawing preceding the last—Number 'FIFTY-ONE' in the twenty-first district of Muscogee, (drawn on the 24th instant by a female ideot [*sic*] of Columbia county,) was this great prize. Every body talked of Number FIFTY-ONE—it was so extremely valuable—it would command so large a price. On Thursday morning expectation was on tip-toe and the speculators kept a sharp look out. An hour or two before the invaluable 'FIFTY ONE' was drawn, another *fifty-one*, in a different district of Muscogee, came out. The sound of number *'fifty-one'* had an electric effect—Every body started and stared—it was, however, No. 51 in the *second*, and not in the twenty-first district, and was drawn by a revolutionary soldier of Jefferson county. Number *fifty-one* had taken so strong a hold on the mind of one of the speculators, that he altogether disregarded the DISTRICT, and leaping upon his horse, was in a moment out of sight, in pursuit of the man of the Revolution; wishing no doubt to experience the pleasure which is afforded to every philanthropic heart in being the *first* to communicate to so worthy a character the *full extent* of his good fortune. The unfortunate mistake of the speculator being discovered almost immediately by his friends, they started after him, instantly, two expresses mounted on fleet horses, with instructions to ride him down and warn him of his error.—But he was not to be overtaken—John Gilpin, in his celebrated London race, did not go faster. In vain did the expresses urge forward their horses, in the hope of getting within hailing distance—the speculator flew before them almost with the swiftness of the wind. In *two hours* he was at Sandersville, a distance of *twenty-seven* miles—getting a fresh horse there, and one or more afterwards, he arrived at his place of destination, at least *sixty-five* miles from Milledgeville, in about *five hours!*—That road was never before travelled with such speed, and perhaps will not be again, until we have another Land Lottery. A bargain for the land was quickly struck and a part of the purchase money paid down, long before the arrival of either of the expresses. We are glad to learn, however, that when the mistake of the buyer had been discovered, the Revolutionary veteran cheerfully returned the money and cancelled the sale."

Research Strategies

Almost every land lottery research question can be answered through one of five plans. These step-by-step processes are designed to simplify the land lottery research process. Each step references more detailed information later in this book. While they lead to the records for most research questions, these strategies do not address every possible record that may pertain to a person or lot.

Researching Land Titles

Obtaining the grant and plat for a land lot won in the land lotteries is a straightforward research task.

Grantee of Whole Lot

Step One:	Locate the lot in the *Index Leading to Page*. Listed by county, district, and land lot, the index includes a reference to the book and page of each lot's recorded grant. See page 58.
Step Two:	Use the page number reference to access the grant book. To locate the referenced grant book, find the corresponding original county in the land lottery chapters beginning on page 77, or the less-common grant books listed on page 61.
Step Three:	Use the land lot number to access the plat. Land Lot plats are recorded in numerical order under their respective district. Locate the plat book under the appropriate original county, beginning on page 77.

Grantee of Fractional Lot

Step One:	Locate the lot in the *Index Leading to Page*. Listed by county, district, and land lot, the index includes a reference to the book and page of each lot's recorded grant. See page 58.
Step Two:	Use the page number reference to access the grant book. See page 59 for fraction grant books. If the index or grant does not identify a grantee, proceed to Step Three.

Step Three:	Locate the lot in the *Fractional Lots Index*. Arranged by county, district, and land lot, the index identifies the grantee for each fraction. See page 57.
Step Four:	If the grantee has not been found at this point, search financial records pertaining to fractional lots. See page 71.
Step Five:	Use the land lot number to access the plat. Land Lot plats are recorded in numerical order under their respective district. See the land lottery chapters from page 77 to locate the plat book for the corresponding district.

Researching Individuals

Individuals can be divided into three primary categories of land lottery participation: participants, fortunate drawers, and purchasers. For the purposes of describing these research strategies, participants are people who registered for draws in the lotteries but did not win. Fortunate drawers are those who won land. Purchasers are people who bought land lots from the state in the years following the land lotteries. Purchasers bought fractional land lots, city lots, and other lots not granted to fortunate drawers. Of the three categories, records of purchasers are the most challenging to find if the land lot number is not already known.

Fortunate Drawers

| **Step One:** | Search published land lottery indexes. See page 40. |
| **Step Two:** | Using the land lot from the published index, locate the record in the *Index Leading to Name*. See page 56. This step is for verification purposes. The index identifies each fortunate drawer, their residence at the time of registration, and the grant date. If a second name is recorded, it means the lot reverted to the state and was sold to someone other than the fortunate drawer. If the lot reverted, your search ends here; there will be no further information about the fortunate drawer. |

Step Three: If the lot was granted to the fortunate drawer, locate the lot's entry in the *Index Leading to Page*. See page 58. Generally, entries only include a page number. This means the book is the district grant book, e.g. Lee County District 7 Grant Book. Grants issued from 1825 to 1829 are recorded in a Supplementary book, identified with "Sup" or "Supplementary." See page 53 for grant book descriptions.

Step Four: Use the page number reference to access the grant book. To locate the referenced grant book, find the corresponding original county in the land lottery chapters beginning on page 77.

Step Five: Use the land lot number to access the plat. Land Lot plats are recorded in numerical order under their respective district. See the land lottery chapters from page 77 to locate the plat book for the corresponding county and district.

Participants

Step One: For the 1805 Land Lottery, search published indexes. See page 31.

Step Two: For other land lotteries, locate county history books which may include transcribed land lottery lists.

Step Three: Search the Periodical Source Index (PERSI) for land lottery list transcriptions published in periodicals.

Step Four: Locate an existing list on microfilm. See page 32.

Purchasers

Step One: Narrow the search to a geographic area, preferably a single land district, or an original county. This may be done by related research in deed and tax records.

Step Two: Browse the *Index Leading to Name* (page 57) and *Fractional Lots Index* (page 56).

Step Three: If the name is found, locate the associated lot in the *Index Leading to Page*. See page 58.

Step Four: Use the page number reference to access the grant book. See page 59 for fraction grant books; the land lottery chapters beginning on page 77 for reverted lot grant books; and other grant books on page 61.

Other Records

Four additional searches may be added to the preceding research plans.

Land Lottery Records collection (page 67). Includes loose documents for many land lots. Perform this search especially if there is an indication that a mistake was made in the grant process or if a legal challenge was made.

Executive Minutes (page 70). Often attached to the grant, executive orders most often correct mistakes on grants. Executive Department Minutes are available on microfilm and are indexed by name and subject.

Laws and Resolutions (page 72). The legislature took action on behalf of numerous individuals to correct legal problems with land lots.

Courts (page 71). Suits involving land lots were most often heard in the county Superior Court. In more rare instances, cases may be found in the Georgia Supreme Court files or federal district court records.

Financial Records (page 71). Records of fees paid for land lots are not indexed but can be particularly useful when researching fractional lot grants.

Participants 4

Almost every citizen of Georgia was eligible for at least one draw in one land lottery. Each authorizing law defined particular categories of participants, such as widows, orphans, or Revolutionary War veterans; no blacks, even free persons of color, could participate. The lists of eligible persons are similar among all the lotteries, but important differences in qualifications can provide vital clues to the life histories of participants. Registration lists include each participant's name and number of draws. Depending on the person performing the registration, there may be a notation with the name identifying the applicable registration category, e.g. R.S. for Revolutionary Soldier.

Each lottery had a distinct registration period. People went to their county courthouse, or local justice of the peace, and paid 12 ½ cents per draw to register. After compiling the county lists, clerks sent the original to the state for the land lottery and kept a copy in the county to be referenced later if problems arose. In practice, these local copies were maintained by the Inferior Court, despite the legal requirement that they be submitted to the Superior Court. As with any event with a deadline, some people registered late. Many counties sent additional names to the state after the first book had been sent. For example, in 1832 names were added to the wheels after the drawing had begun.

The 1805 Land Lottery List of Persons Entitled to Draws is a special case. For the first lottery, the state commissioners wrote the name of every participant in a single set of volumes. These names were then read in order at the lottery and prize tickets were drawn from a box as each name was called. The 1805 lottery record is the only complete list of participants available for any of the Georgia land lotteries. It is available on microfilm and in published form. Lists of participants from other land lotteries have been published in periodicals. Use the Periodical Source Index (PERSI) available at many public libraries on CD-ROM or through HeritageQuest Online.

Graham, Paul K. *1805 Georgia Land Lottery Persons Entitled to Draws.* Decatur, Ga.: The Genealogy Company, 2005.

Wood, Virginia S. and Ralph V. Wood. *1805 Georgia Land Lottery.* Cambridge, Mass.: Greenwood Press, 1964.

Records of Participants

The table below identifies lists of persons entitled to draws available at the Georgia Archives, with the exception of the 1807 list from Hancock County. It is not meant to be a comprehensive record of every list of participants, some having never been filmed. The state-wide 1805 lottery list is available in Georgia Archives microfilm drawer 90, box 42.

County	Land Lottery	Ga. Archives Microfilm
Baldwin	1820	Drawer 199, Box 73
Baldwin	1821	Drawer 139, Box 71
Chatham	1832	Drawer 20, Box 54
Columbia	1805, 1807	Drawer 48, Box 79
Columbia	1821 (partial)	Drawer 48, Box 80
Elbert	1807, 1821, 1827, 1832	Drawer 10, Box 83
Elbert	1821	Drawer 2, Box 77
Franklin	1820	Original list in DOC-4826
Franklin	1821	Original list in DOC-4833
Greene	1807, 1827, 1832	Drawer 230, Box 1
Greene	1832 (partial)	Drawer 109, Box 9
Hancock	1805, 1820, 1821, 1827	Drawer 142, Box 48
Hancock	1807	in county courthouse
Hancock	1832	Drawer 50, Box 77
Jackson	1807, 1827, 1832	Drawer 171, Box 24
Jefferson	1827, 1832	Drawer 22, Box 62
Jones	1820, 1821, 1827, 1832	Drawer 76, Box 65
Laurens	1820	Drawer 119, Box 72
Meriwether	1832	Drawer 281, Box 66
Morgan	1827 (incomplete)	Drawer 42, Box 67
Oglethorpe	1805, 1807, 1820, 1832	Drawer 71, Box 36

Continued next page...

County	Land Lottery	Ga. Archives Microfilm
Oglethorpe	1807, 1820, 1832	Drawer 47, Box 18
Pulaski	1832	Drawer 39, Box 43
Taliaferro	1832	Drawer 109, Box 9
Wilkes	*all*	Drawer 45, Box 19

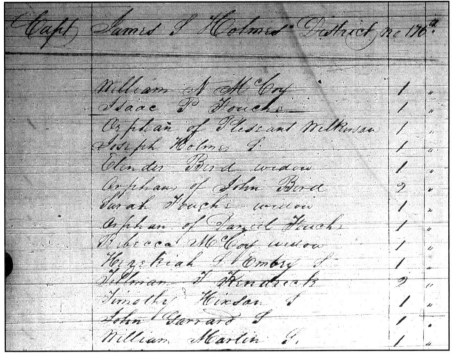

Figure 8. List of Persons Entitled to Draws, 1832 Lottery, Wilkes County

Qualifications

Qualifications for participation varied by land lottery. The lists have been published in numerous locations, including the land lottery books listed in the next chapter of this book. Qualifications and restrictions found in lottery laws are in narrative form and much of the nuance is lost when the sentences are broken out and displayed in list form. Researchers who use the lists of qualifications to prove a genealogical case should consult the original laws rather than condensed lists like those found here.

This book's land lottery chapters include lists of qualifications for participation. See the following pages for each lottery.

Qualification Categories

The following list shows the years each qualification category was used. Due to the complexity of land lottery laws, the list does not include all possible reasons to explain why a person may or may not have participated in the land lotteries. It is meant only to guide the researcher to each lottery law for more detailed explanation.

All	1805	1807	1820	1821	1827	1832 Land	1832 Gold
White	●	●	●	●	●	●	●
U.S. Citizen	●	●	●	●	●	●	●
Georgia resident, 1 year	●						
Georgia resident, 3 years		●	●	●	●	●	●
Deaf, dumb, and blind, not having won previously						●	

Men

	1805	1807	1820	1821	1827	1832 Land	1832 Gold
Age 21, single or with family	●	●					
Age 18, single or with family			●	●	●	●	●
Age 18, having previously won as orphan					●	●	

Women

	1805	1807	1820	1821	1827	1832 Land	1832 Gold
Widow with children	●						
Widow		●	●	●	●	●	●
Single woman, age 21		●					
Widow, husband killed in Revolution, War of 1812, or against Indians			●	●			
Widow, husband killed or died in Revolution, War of 1812, or against Indians					●	●	
Age 18, having previously won as orphan					●	●	
Wife of man absent from state for 3 years					●	●	
Single woman, age 18, father killed or died in Revolution, War of 1812, or against Indians						●	
Widow of Revolutionary veteran					●	●	
Widow of veteran of Indian wars, 1784-1797						●	

Children

Children	1805	1807	1820	1821	1827	1832 Land	1832 Gold
Orphan or orphan family	•	•	•	•	•	•	•
Orphan family that won in previous lottery			•			•	•
Orphan family, father killed in Revolution, War of 1812, or against Indians			•	•			
Orphan family, father killed or died in Revolution, War of 1812, or against Indians			•	•			
Child(ren) of convict in penitentiary						•	•
Age 10 to 17, idiot, lunatic, insane, blind, deaf, dumb						•	•
Illegitimate child(ren)						•	•
Child(ren) of man absent from state for 3 years							•

Military

Military	1805	1807	1820	1821	1827	1832 Land	1832 Gold
Revolutionary or War of 1812 veteran, indigent or invalid			•				
Recent military draftee not meeting residence requirement			•				
Indigent or invalid veteran of Revolution or War of 1812 who won in previous lottery			•				
Disabled veteran of War of 1812					•		
Revolutionary veteran					•	•	

Military

Military	1805	1807	1820	1821	1827	1832 Land	1832 Gold
Veteran, War of 1812 or Indians					•	•	
Veteran, even if winner in previous lottery						•	
Veteran of Indian wars, 1784-1797						•	
Man who paid for substitute, War of 1812						•	

Excluded Persons

Excluded Persons	1805	1807	1820	1821	1827	1832 Land	1832 Gold
Winner in previous lottery		•	•	•	•	•	
Person who evaded draft			•	•	•	•	•
Deserter				•	•		
Debt absconder				•	•		
Tax defaulter				•	•		
Left state to avoid laws				•	•	•	
Convict in penitentiary				•	•	•	
Anyone "directly or indirectly concerned" with the Pony Club (gang of thieves)						•	
Convicted felon						•	

Excluded Persons	1805	1807	1820	1821	1827	1832 Land	1832 Gold
Mining gold in Cherokee Territory from 1 January 1830						•	
Living in Cherokee Territory						•	

All eight land lottery drawings followed the same basic procedure. Names were placed in one wheel and lot numbers were placed in another. Names drawn with a lot were considered "fortunate drawers," giving the person an exclusive opportunity to obtain a grant to the land. In the first three lotteries, blank tickets were added to lot tickets to equal the total number of name tickets. That process became cumbersome as the number of participants increased. From the 1821 lottery forward, lots and names were drawn until all the lot tickets were exhausted.

At the 1805 Land Lottery names were written in a book rather than on tickets. As each name was read, a "prize" or "blank" ticket was pulled from a box. If a prize ticket was drawn, the lottery commissioners wrote information in three separate books. First, a "P" notation was made in the List of Persons Entitled to Draws, designating a prize. Next, the prize result was written in a separate book in the order in which the lots were drawn. Third, the prize result was written in a volume arranged by land lot number.

Beginning in 1807, names were written on tickets and drawn against lot tickets. When a name matched a lot, it was written down in two books. One book was arranged by land lot and the fortunate drawer's name was written on the appropriate line. These were known as Numerical Books, now identified as the Index Leading to Name at the Georgia Archives. Another book was arranged by county, then letter of last name. Names were written on the appropriate page as they were drawn. These were known as the Alphabetical Books. Today, derivatives of the Numerical Books and the original Alphabetical Books form the basis for researching fortunate drawers. Copies of the original Numerical Books have been microfilmed and are found under the title "Index Leading to Name" (see page 56). The Alphabetical Books have not been microfilmed.

Records of Fortunate Drawers

Published Indexes

1805 Land Lottery

> Graham, Paul K. *1805 Georgia Land Lottery Fortunate Drawers and Grantees.* Decatur, Ga.: The Genealogy Company, 2004.

1807 Land Lottery

> Lucas, Silas Emmett, Jr. *The Second or 1807 Land Lottery of Georgia.* Easly, S.C.: Southern Historical Press, 1986.

1820 Land Lottery

> Lucas, Silas Emmett, Jr. *The Third or 1820 Land Lottery of Georgia.* Easly, S.C.: Southern Historical Press, 1986.

1821 Land Lottery

> Lucas, Silas Emmett, Jr. *The Fourth or 1821 Land Lottery of Georgia.* Easley, S.C.: Southern Historical Press, 1986.

1827 Land Lottery

> Houston, Martha Lou. *Reprint of Official Register of Land Lottery of Georgia 1827.* 1928. Reprint, Easley, S.C.: Southern Historical Press, 1986.

1832 Land Lottery

> Smith, James F., *The Cherokee Land Lottery.* 1838. Reprint, Greenville, S.C.: Southern Historical Press, 1991.

1832 Gold Lottery

> Lucas, S. Emmett, Jr. *The 1832 Gold Lottery of Georgia.* Easley, S.C.: Southern Historical Press, 1988.
> Warren, Mary Bondurant. *Alphabetical Index to Georgia's 1832 Gold Lottery.* Danielsville, Ga.: Heritage Papers, 1981.

Davis, Robert S., Jr. *The 1833 Land Lottery of Georgia and Other Missing Names of Winners in the Georgia Land Lotteries.* Greenville, S.C.: Southern Historical Press, 1991.

Lists of Fortunate Drawers (Alphabetical Books)

These books, compiled at the time of each land lottery drawing, were used to create the published indexes for every lottery except the 1827 and 1832 land lotteries (above). They are arranged by lottery, then county, then by first letter of the surname. The following list includes references to all of the Alphabetical Book volumes, listed by county, then lottery. For the 1805 Land Lottery, researchers should use the List of Persons Entitled to Draws (page 59). Three columns identify the county, the land lotteries, and the Georgia Archives record number for the book. The record number is included here to expedite the research process but is not used in citations.

County	Land Lottery	Record Number
Appling	1820	DOC-4824
	1821	DOC-4831
	1827	DOC-4838
	1832 Gold	DOC-4857
	1832 Land	DOC-4846
Baker	1827	DOC-4838
	1832 Gold	DOC-4857
	1832 Land	DOC-4846
Baldwin	1807	DOC-4820
	1820	DOC-4824
	1821	DOC-4831
	1827	DOC-4838
	1832 Gold	DOC-4857
	1832 Land	DOC-4846
Bibb	1827	DOC-4838
	1832 Gold	DOC-4857

County	Land Lottery	Record Number
Bibb	1832 Land	DOC-4846
Bryan	1807	DOC-4820
	1820	DOC-4824
	1821	DOC-4831
	1827	DOC-4838
	1832 Gold	DOC-4857
	1832 Land	DOC-4846
Bulloch	1807	DOC-4820
	1820	DOC-4824
	1821	DOC-4831
	1827	DOC-4838
	1832 Gold	DOC-4857
	1832 Land	DOC-4846
Burke	1807	DOC-4820
	1820	DOC-4824
	1821	DOC-4831
	1827	DOC-4838
	1832 Gold	DOC-4857
	1832 Land	DOC-4846
Butts	1827	DOC-4838
	1832 Gold	DOC-4857
	1832 Land	DOC-4846
Camden	1807	DOC-4820
	1820	DOC-4824
	1821	DOC-4831
	1827	DOC-4838
	1832 Gold	DOC-4858
	1832 Land	DOC-4847
Campbell	1832 Gold	DOC-4858
	1832 Land	DOC-4847
Carroll	1832 Gold	DOC-4858
	1832 Land	DOC-4847

County	Land Lottery	Record Number
Chatham	1807	DOC-4820
	1820	DOC-4825
	1821	DOC-4831
	1827	DOC-4839
	1832 Gold	DOC-4858
	1832 Land	DOC-4847
Cherokee	1832 Gold	DOC-4858
	1832 Land	DOC-4847
Clarke	1807	DOC-4820
	1820	DOC-4825
	1821	DOC-4832
	1827	DOC-4839
	1832 Gold	DOC-4858
	1832 Land	DOC-4847
Columbia	1807	DOC-4820
	1820	DOC-4825
	1821	DOC-4832
	1827	DOC-4839
	1832 Gold	DOC-4858
	1832 Land	DOC-4847
Coweta	1832 Gold	DOC-4858
	1832 Land	DOC-4848
Crawford	1827	DOC-4839
	1832 Gold	DOC-4859
	1832 Land	DOC-4848
Decatur	1827	DOC-4839
	1832 Gold	DOC-4859
	1832 Land	DOC-4848
DeKalb	1827	DOC-4839
	1832 Gold	DOC-4859
	1832 Land	DOC-4848

County	Land Lottery	Record Number
Dooly	1827	DOC-4839
	1832 Gold	DOC-4859
	1832 Land	DOC-4848
Early	1820	DOC-4825
	1821	DOC-4832
	1827	DOC-4839
	1832 Gold	DOC-4859
	1832 Land	DOC-4848
Effingham	1807	DOC-4821
	1820	DOC-4825
	1821	DOC-4832
	1827	DOC-4839
	1832 Gold	DOC-4859
	1832 Land	DOC-4848
Elbert	1807	DOC-4821
	1820	DOC-4825
	1821	DOC-4832
	1827	DOC-4840
	1832 Gold	DOC-4859
	1832 Land	DOC-4848
Emanuel	1820	DOC-4826
	1821	DOC-4832
	1827	DOC-4840
	1832 Gold	DOC-4859
	1832 Land	DOC-4848
Fayette	1827	DOC-4840
	1832 Gold	DOC-4860
	1832 Land	DOC-4849
Franklin	1807	DOC-4821
	1820	DOC-4826
	1821	DOC-4833
	1827	DOC-4840
	1832 Gold	DOC-4860

County	Land Lottery	Record Number
Franklin	1832 Land	DOC-4849
Glynn	1807	DOC-4821
	1820	DOC-4826
	1821	DOC-4833
	1827	DOC-4840
	1832 Gold	DOC-4860
	1832 Land	DOC-4849
Greene	1807	DOC-4821
	1820	DOC-4826
	1821	DOC-4833
	1827	DOC-4840
	1832 Gold	DOC-4860
	1832 Land	DOC-4849
Gwinnett	1820	DOC-4826
	1821	DOC-4833
	1827	DOC-4840
	1832 Gold	DOC-4860
	1832 Land	DOC-4849
Habersham	1820	DOC-4827
	1821	DOC-4833
	1827	DOC-4840
	1832 Gold	DOC-4860
	1832 Land	DOC-4849
Hall	1820	DOC-4826
	1821	DOC-4833
	1827	DOC-4841
	1832 Gold	DOC-4861
	1832 Land	DOC-4850
Hancock	1807	DOC-4821
	1820	DOC-4827
	1821	DOC-4834
	1827	DOC-4841
	1832 Gold	DOC-4861

County	Land Lottery	Record Number
Hancock	1832 Land	DOC-4850
Harris	1832 Gold	DOC-4861
	1832 Land	DOC-4850
Heard	1832 Gold	DOC-4861
	1832 Land	DOC-4850
Henry	1827	DOC-4841
	1832 Gold	DOC-4861
	1832 Land	DOC-4850
Houston	1827	DOC-4841
	1832 Gold	DOC-4861
	1832 Land	DOC-4850
Irwin	1820	DOC-4827
	1821	DOC-4834
	1827	DOC-4841
	1832 Gold	DOC-4861
	1832 Land	DOC-4850
Jackson	1807	DOC-4821
	1820	DOC-4827
	1821	DOC-4834
	1827	DOC-4841
	1832 Gold	DOC-4862
	1832 Land	DOC-4851
Jasper	1820	DOC-4827
	1821	DOC-4834
	1827	DOC-4841
	1832 Gold	DOC-4862
	1832 Land	DOC-4851
Jefferson	1807	DOC-4821
	1820	DOC-4827
	1821	DOC-4834
	1827	DOC-4841
	1832 Gold	DOC-4862

County	Land Lottery	Record Number
Jefferson	1832 Land	DOC-4851
Jones	1820	DOC-4827
	1821	DOC-4834
	1827	DOC-4842
	1832 Gold	DOC-4862
	1832 Land	DOC-4851
Laurens	1820	DOC-4828
	1821	DOC-4834
	1827	DOC-4842
	1832 Gold	DOC-4862
	1832 Land	DOC-4851
Lee	1832 Gold	DOC-4862
	1832 Land	DOC-4851
Liberty	1807	DOC-4821
	1820	DOC-4828
	1821	DOC-4835
	1827	DOC-4842
	1832 Gold	DOC-4862
	1832 Land	DOC-4851
Lincoln	1807	DOC-4821
	1820	DOC-4828
	1821	DOC-4835
	1827	DOC-4842
	1832 Gold	DOC-4863
	1832 Land	DOC-4852
Lowndes	1832 Gold	DOC-4863
	1832 Land	DOC-4852
Madison	1820	DOC-4828
	1821	DOC-4835
	1827	DOC-4842
	1832 Gold	DOC-4863
	1832 Land	DOC-4852

County	Land Lottery	Record Number
Marion	1832 Gold	DOC-4863
	1832 Land	DOC-4852
McIntosh	1807	DOC-4822
	1820	DOC-4828
	1821	DOC-4835
	1827	DOC-4842
	1832 Gold	DOC-4863
	1832 Land	DOC-4852
Meriwether	1832 Gold	DOC-4863
	1832 Land	DOC-4852
Monroe	1827	DOC-4842
	1832 Gold	DOC-4863
	1832 Land	DOC-4852
Montgomery	1807	DOC-4822
	1820	DOC-4828
	1821	DOC-4835
	1827	DOC-4843
	1832 Gold	DOC-482
	1832 Land	DOC-4853
Morgan	1820	DOC-4828
	1821	DOC-4835
	1827	DOC-4843
	1832 Gold	DOC-482
	1832 Land	DOC-4853
Muscogee	1832 Gold	DOC-482
	1832 Land	DOC-4853
Newton	1827	DOC-4843
	1832 Gold	DOC-482
	1832 Land	DOC-4853
Oglethorpe	1807	DOC-4822
	1820	DOC-4829
	1821	DOC-4835

County	Land Lottery	Record Number
Oglethorpe	1827	DOC-4843
	1832 Gold	DOC-482
	1832 Land	DOC-4853
Pike	1827	DOC-4843
	1832 Gold	DOC-482
	1832 Land	DOC-4853
Pulaski	1820	DOC-4829
	1821	DOC-4836
	1827	DOC-4843
	1832 Gold	DOC-482
	1832 Land	DOC-4853
Putnam	1820	DOC-4829
	1821	DOC-4836
	1827	DOC-4843
	1832 Gold	DOC-4864
	1832 Land	DOC-4854
Rabun	1821	DOC-4836
	1827	DOC-4844
	1832 Gold	DOC-4864
	1832 Land	DOC-4854
Randolph	1832 Gold	DOC-4864
	1832 Land	DOC-4854
Richmond	1807	DOC-4822
	1820	DOC-4829
	1821	DOC-4836
	1827	DOC-4844
	1832 Gold	DOC-4864
	1832 Land	DOC-4854
Screven	1807	DOC-4822
	1820	DOC-4829
	1821	DOC-4836
	1827	DOC-4844

County	Land Lottery	Record Number
Screven	1832 Gold	DOC-4864
	1832 Land	DOC-4854
Stewart	1832 Gold	DOC-4864
	1832 Land	DOC-4854
Sumter	1832 Gold	DOC-4864
	1832 Land	DOC-4854
Talbot	1832 Gold	DOC-4865
	1832 Land	DOC-4855
Taliaferro	1827	DOC-4844
	1832 Gold	DOC-4865
	1832 Land	DOC-4855
Tattnall	1807	DOC-4822
	1820	DOC-4829
	1821	DOC-4836
	1827	DOC-4844
	1832 Gold	DOC-4865
	1832 Land	DOC-4855
Telfair	1820	DOC-4829
	1821	DOC-4836
	1827	DOC-4844
	1832 Gold	DOC-4865
	1832 Land	DOC-4855
Thomas	1827	DOC-4844
	1832 Gold	DOC-4865
	1832 Land	DOC-4855
Troup	1832 Gold	DOC-4865
	1832 Land	DOC-4855
Twiggs	1820	DOC-4830
	1821	DOC-4837
	1827	DOC-4844
	1832 Gold	DOC-4865

County	Land Lottery	Record Number
Twiggs	1832 Land	DOC-4855
Upson	1827	DOC-4845
	1832 Gold	DOC-4866
	1832 Land	DOC-4856
Walton	1820	DOC-4830
	1821	DOC-4837
	1827	DOC-4845
	1832 Gold	DOC-4866
	1832 Land	DOC-4856
Ware	1827	DOC-4845
	1832 Gold	DOC-4866
	1832 Land	DOC-4856
Warren	1807	DOC-4822
	1820	DOC-4830
	1821	DOC-4837
	1827	DOC-4845
	1832 Gold	DOC-4866
	1832 Land	DOC-4856
Washington	1807	DOC-4822
	1820	DOC-4830
	1821	DOC-4837
	1827	DOC-4845
	1832 Gold	DOC-4866
	1832 Land	DOC-4856
Wayne	1807	DOC-4822
	1820	DOC-4830
	1832 Gold	DOC-4866
	1832 Land	DOC-4856
Wilkes	1807	DOC-4822
	1820	DOC-4830
	1821	DOC-4837
	1827	DOC-4845

County	Land Lottery	Record Number
Wilkes	1832 Gold	DOC-4866
	1832 Land	DOC-4856
Wilkinson	1807	DOC-4822
	1820	DOC-4830
	1821	DOC-4837
	1827	DOC-4845
	1832 Gold	DOC-4866
	1832 Land	DOC-4856

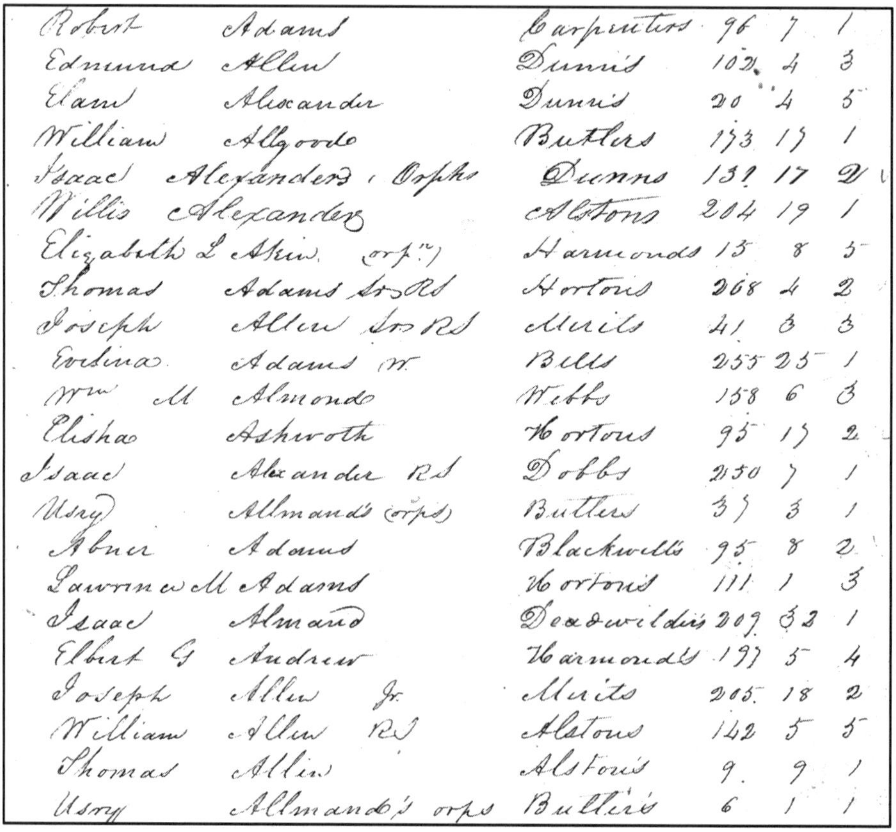

Robert	Adams	Carpenters	96	7	1
Edmund	Allen	Dunn's	102	4	3
Elam	Alexander	Dunn's	20	4	5
William	Allgood	Butlers	173	17	1
Isaac	Alexanders Orphs	Dunns	131	17	2
Willis	Alexander	Alstons	204	19	1
Elizabeth L	Atkin (orp)	Hammonds	15	8	5
Thomas	Adams Srs RS	Hortons	268	4	2
Joseph	Allen Srs RS	Merils	41	3	3
Evelina	Adams W	Bells	255	25	1
Wm M	Almond	Webbs	158	6	3
Elisha	Ashworth	Hortons	95	17	2
Isaac	Alexander RS	Dobbs	250	7	1
Usry	Allmand's (orps)	Butlers	37	3	1
Abner	Adams	Blackwells	95	8	2
Lawrence M	Adams	Hortons	111	1	3
Isaac	Almand	Deadwilders	207	32	1
Elbert G	Andrew	Hammonds	197	5	4
Joseph	Allen Jr	Merits	205	18	2
William	Allen RS	Alstons	142	5	5
Thomas	Allen	Alstons	9	9	1
Usry	Allmand's orps	Butlers	6	1	1

Figure 9. List of Fortunate Drawers, 1820 Land Lottery, Early County

Grants 6

Grants are the legal instrument that transfers land title from the sovereign government (Georgia) to an individual or corporate body. Grants in Georgia take many forms, but all serve the purpose of title transfer. Grants are important because they identify the first private owner of each tract of land.

There were three ways an individual could obtain a grant in the land lottery or reserve areas of the state. First, they could take out a grant on the lot they won in the lottery. Second, they could purchase a lot from the state, such as a fractional or reverted lot. Third, they could bring suit against a fortunate drawer who registered fraudulently. In the latter case, if a jury found the defendant guilty, the plaintiff received half the land lot as a reward.

Georgia's land lottery grant books are arranged by the type of grant and the land's geographic location. The vast majority of land lottery grants are made to the fortunate drawers. Of those, most are recorded in **District Grant Books**. Each district grant book contains the grants issued to fortunate drawers within one land district. For example, land granted to fortunate drawers in Coweta County, District 8, can be found in the Coweta County District 8 Grant Book. Often, two district grant books are recorded in the same physical volume. Each volume contains a comprehensive name index at the front, but grants for each district are recorded in separate sections. Page numbers for the second district in the volume start again at one.

From 1825 to 1829, Georgia claimed mineral rights and grant books reflected the change in legal language. These **Supplementary Books** contain grants to fortunate drawers during that particular four year period. When the Georgia legislature repealed the mineral rights law in 1829, it gave all people with supplementary grants rights to the minerals under their land. Supplementary books generally cover one or more original counties in a single volume, e.g., Walton County Supplementary Book.

Other books contain grants issued to people who did not win in the land lotteries. **Fractions Grant Books** contain grants to fractional lots that were held out of each lottery and sold at a later date. There are fourteen fractions grant books lettered A through N and HH. Each book corresponds to fractional lots granted under a specific act of the legislature. Fractions in the 1833 Fractions Lottery are recorded in district grant books rather than fractions grant books. **Reverted Lots Grant Books** contain grants to lots won in a land lottery but not granted to the fortunate drawer. The legislature continually extended the time allowed for fortunate drawers to take out grants but eventually brought the extensions to an end. The dates that reverted lots began to be sold are listed in the land lottery chapters at the end of this book. Reverted lots grant books are arranged by lottery; districts with many reverted lots have their own book.

Grants recorded in the **Forfeited Land Grant Book** were purchased from the state, but the purchaser failed to pay all the required fees. The lots were sold at auction to new buyers who ultimately obtained a grant. Almost all forfeited lands are located in original Appling County, districts twelve and thirteen. The **Relinquished Lots Grant Book** includes grants for land actively given up by the fortunate drawer. Fortunate drawers who knew they were not going to take out a grant on the land could write to the Secretary of State and relinquish their lot to the state. Some relinquished lots were drawn in the 1833 Fractions Lottery. Others were sold at sheriff's sales. Grants to lots condemned as fraudulently drawn are recorded in **Fraudulent Draws Grant Books**. The **Miscellaneous Lots Grant Book** contains uncategorized grants made under unique circumstances.

For information about the three most common grant books, see the land lottery chapters at the conclusion of this volume, beginning on page 77.

District Grant Books
Supplementary Grant Books
Reverted Lots Grant Books

For information about the remaining grant books, see pages 59 to 61.

Fractions Grant Books
Forfeited Land Grant Book
Relinquished Lots Grant Book
Fraudulent Draws Grant Books
Miscellaneous Lots Grant Book

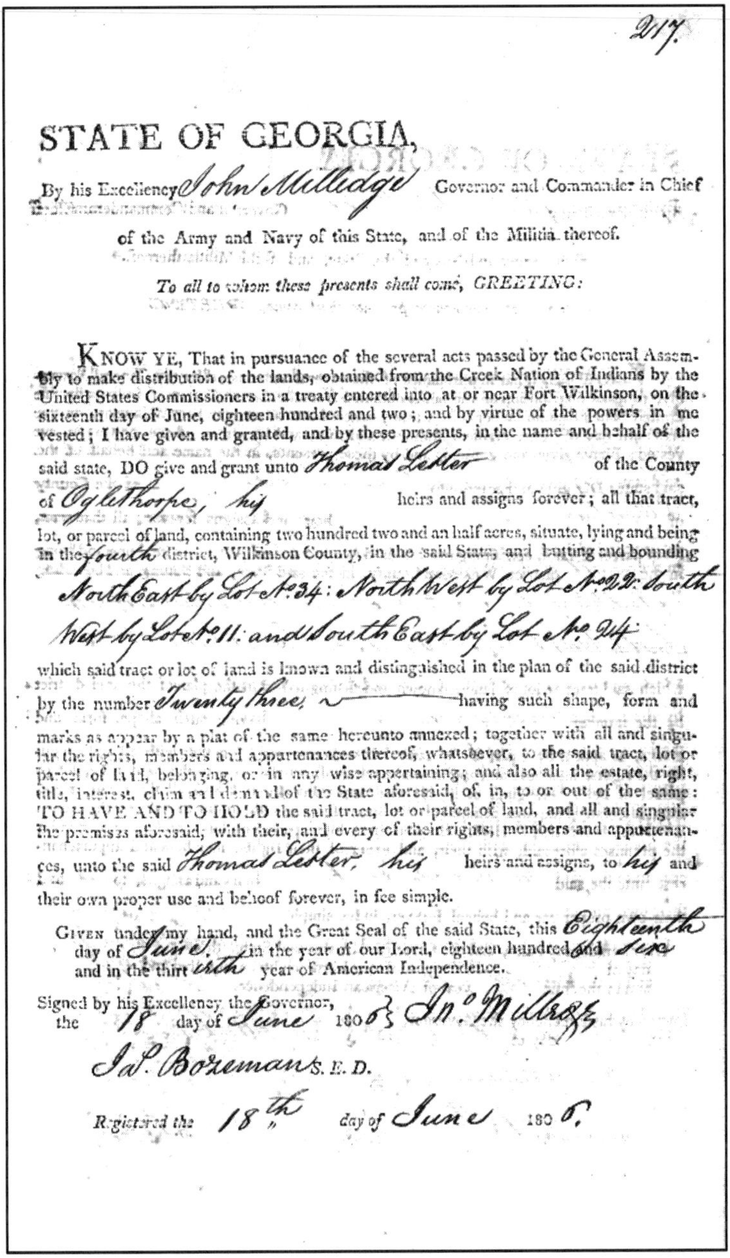

217.

STATE OF GEORGIA,

By his Excellency *John Milledge* Governor and Commander in Chief

of the Army and Navy of this State, and of the Militia thereof.

To all to whom these presents shall come, GREETING:

KNOW YE, That in pursuance of the several acts passed by the General Assembly to make distribution of the lands, obtained from the Creek Nation of Indians by the United States Commissioners in a treaty entered into at or near Fort Wilkinson, on the sixteenth day of June, eighteen hundred and two; and by virtue of the powers in me vested; I have given and granted, and by these presents, in the name and behalf of the said state, DO give and grant unto *Thomas Lester* of the County of *Oglethorpe, his* heirs and assigns forever; all that tract, lot, or parcel of land, containing two hundred two and a half acres, situate, lying and being in the *fourth* district, Wilkinson County, in the said State, and butting and bounding *North East by Lot No. 34; North West by Lot No. 22; South West by Lot No. 11; and South East by Lot No. 24;* which said tract or lot of land is known and distinguished in the plan of the said district by the number *Twenty three;* having such shape, form and marks as appear by a plat of the same hereunto annexed; together with all and singular the rights, members and appurtenances thereof, whatsoever, to the said tract, lot or parcel of land, belonging, or in any wise appertaining; and also all the estate, right, title, interest, claim and demand of the State aforesaid, of, in, to or out of the same: TO HAVE AND TO HOLD the said tract, lot or parcel of land, and all and singular the premises aforesaid, with their, and every of their rights, members and appurtenances, unto the said *Thomas Lester, his* heirs and assigns, to *his* and their own proper use and behoof forever, in fee simple.

GIVEN under my hand, and the Great Seal of the said State, this *Eighteenth* day of *June,* in the year of our Lord, eighteen hundred and *six* and in the thirt*ieth* year of American Independence.

Signed by his Excellency the Governor, the *18* day of *June* 180*6* *Jno. Milledge*

Jas. Bozeman S. E. D.

Registered the *18th* day of *June* 180*6.*

Figure 10. Grant for land in original Wilkinson County.

Indexes

There are three primary indexes to land lot grants. One lists the grantees and grant dates for all lots drawn in the lotteries. A second lists the grantees and grant dates for fractional lots. The third index specifies the book and page of all recorded land lot grants.

Index Leading to Name

Known historically as the Numerical Books, this multi-volume index is arranged geographically: by county, district, and land lot. It lists the grantee and grant date for each lot drawn in the lotteries, along with various notes and comments added by later clerks. Consult this index to determine if the fortunate drawer took out a grant to the lot.

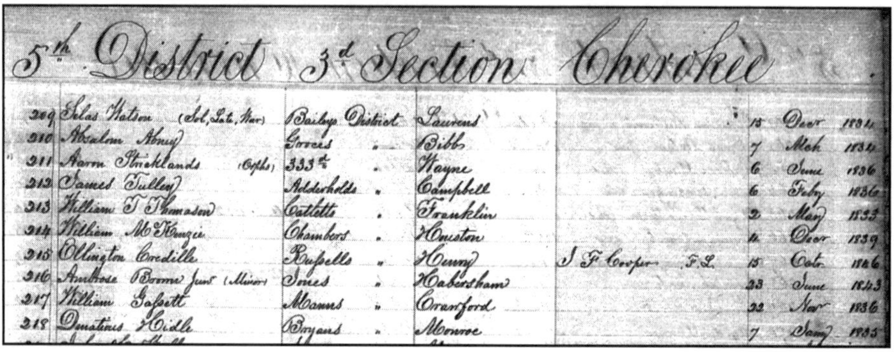

Figure 11. Index Leading to Name, 1832 Land Lottery, Cherokee County

County	Ga. Archives Microfilm
Appling	Drawer 286, Box 46
Baldwin	Drawer 286, Box 45
Carroll	Drawer 286, Box 47
Cherokee, Gold Districts	Drawer 286, Box 48
Cherokee, Land Districts, Sections 1-2	Drawer 286, Box 48
Cherokee, Land Districts, Sections 3-4	Drawer 286, Box 49
Coweta, Dooly	Drawer 286, Box 47
Early, Fayette, Gwinnett	Drawer 286, Box 46
Habersham, Hall, Henry	Drawer 286, Box 46
Houston	Drawer 286, Box 47
Irwin	Drawer 286, Box 46

County	Ga. Archives Microfilm
Lee	Drawer 286, Box 47
Monroe	Drawer 286, Box 46
Muscogee	Drawer 286, Box 47
Rabun	Drawer 286, Box 46
Troup	Drawer 286, Box 47
Walton	Drawer 286, Box 46
Wayne, Wilkinson	Drawer 286, Box 45

Fractional Lots Index

Also arranged numerically, this index identifies the grantees of fractions. Because no comprehensive name index to fractional lot grantees is available, these lists are the best source for ascertaining the names of individuals who purchased fractions.

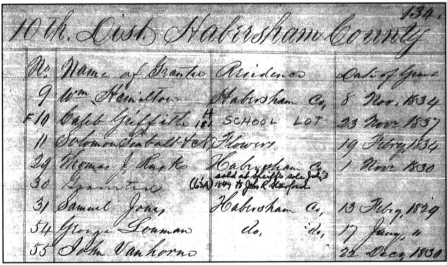

Figure 12. Fractional Lots Index, 1820 Land Lottery, Habersham County

Fractions Index	Ga. Archives Microfilm
1805, 1807, 1820, 1821, 1827	Drawer 286, Box 43
1832 Land, 1832 Gold	Drawer 286, Box 49

Index Leading to Page

The Index Leading to Page identifies the book and page of each recorded land lot grant. It is arranged geographically like the other two indexes. For grants recorded in district grant books, each entry identifies the land lot and page number. Page headers identifying the county and district lead to the corresponding grant book. Grants recorded in other types of books are noted as such, generally by the following abbreviations. "Forfeited" lot grants are identified without abbreviation. See Figure 13 for a sample page from this index.

Abbreviation	Meaning
Frac	Fraction
Revt	Reverted
Sup	Supplementary
Fraud	Fraudulent

County	Ga. Archives Microfilm
Appling, Baldwin	Drawer 286, Box 43
Carroll	Drawer 286, Box 44
Cherokee	Drawer 286, Box 45
Coweta, Dooly	Drawer 286, Box 44
Early	Drawer 286, Box 43
Fayette, Gwinnett	Drawer 286, Box 44
Habersham, Hall, Henry	Drawer 286, Box 44
Houston, Irwin, Lee	Drawer 286, Box 44
Monroe, Muscogee	Drawer 286, Box 44
Rabun, Troup, Walton	Drawer 286, Box 44
Wayne, Wilkinson	Drawer 286, Box 43

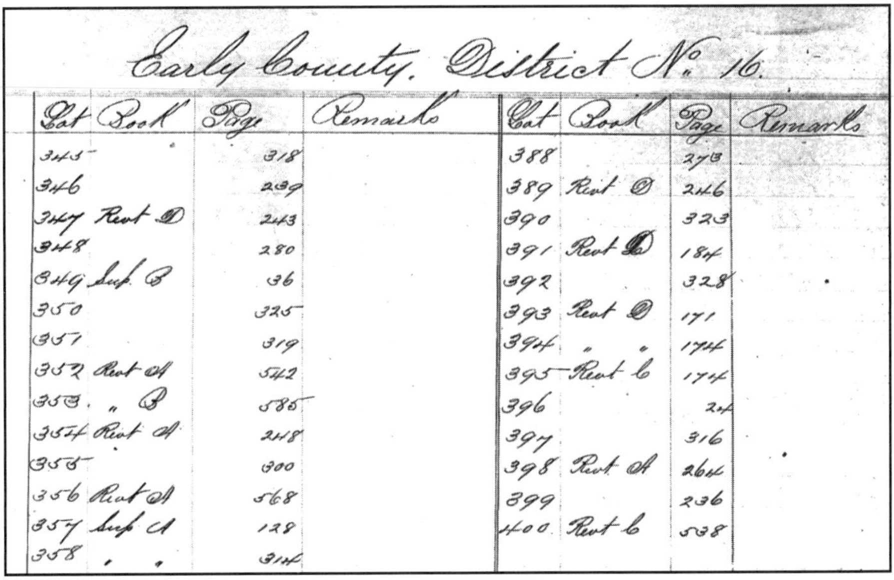

Early County. District No. 16.							
Lot	Book	Page	Remarks	Lot	Book	Page	Remarks
345		318		388		273	
346		239		389	Revt C	246	
347	Revt D	243		390		323	
348		280		391	Revt D	184	
349	Sup. B	36		392		328	
350		325		393	Revt D	171	
351		319		394	" "	174	
352	Revt A	542		395	Revt C	174	
353	" B	585		396		24	
354	Revt A	248		397		316	
355		300		398	Revt A	264	
356	Revt A	568		399		236	
357	Sup. A	128		400	Revt C	538	
358	" "	314					

Figure 13. Index Leading to Page, 1820 Land Lottery, Early County

Grant Books

Most grants were made to fortunate drawers and recorded in district grant books. Lists of these grant books can be found in the land lottery chapters beginning on page 77. The following list includes books for lots granted under separate processes and legal language than the district and supplementary grant books. Many of these grant books contain documents relating to multiple land lotteries.

Fractions Grant Books

Book A: grants for lots held from the 1805 Land Lottery. Georgia Archives microfilm, drawer 286, box 4.

Book B: grants for lots held from the 1807 Land Lottery located in Wilkinson County. Georgia Archives microfilm, drawer 286, box 5.

Book C: grants for lots held from the 1807 Land Lottery located in Baldwin County. Georgia Archives microfilm, drawer 286, box 5.

Book D: grants for lots held from the 1820 Land Lottery located in Irwin, Early, Hall, and Walton counties. Georgia Archives microfilm, drawer 286, box 6.

Book E: grants for lots held from the 1820 Land Lottery located in Appling, Gwinnett, Habersham, Hall, and Rabun counties. Georgia Archives microfilm, drawer 286, box 6.

Book F: grants for lots held from both the 1820 and 1821 land lotteries located in the following counties: Appling, Dooly, Early, Fayette, Gwinnett, Habersham, Hall, Henry, Houston, Irwin, Monroe, Rabun, and Walton. Georgia Archives microfilm, drawer 286, box 7.

Book G: grants for lots held from the 1820 Land Lottery located in Gwinnett, Habersham, Hall, Rabun, and Walton counties. Georgia Archives microfilm, drawer 286, box 7.

Book H: grants for lots held from both the 1820 and 1821 land lotteries located in the following counties: Appling, Dooly, Early, Fayette, Gwinnett, Habersham, Hall, Henry, Houston, Irwin, Monroe, Rabun, and Walton. Georgia Archives microfilm, drawer 286, box 8.

Book I: grants for lots held from the 1820 Land Lottery located in Gwinnett, Habersham, Hall, Rabun, and Walton counties. Georgia Archives microfilm, drawer 286, box 8.

Book K: grants for lots held from the 1820, 1821, and 1827 land lotteries located in the following counties: Appling, Carroll, Coweta, Dooly, Early, Fayette, Gwinnett, Habersham, Hall, Henry, Houston, Irwin, Lee, Monroe, Muscogee, Rabun, Troup, and Walton. Georgia Archives microfilm, drawer 286, box 8.

Book L: grants for lots held from the 1827 Land Lottery located in Carroll, Coweta, Muscogee, Troup, and Lee counties. Georgia Archives microfilm, drawer 286, box 9.

Book M: grants for lots held from all land lotteries. Georgia Archives microfilm, drawer 286, box 9.

Book N: grants for lots held from all land lotteries. Georgia Archives microfilm, drawer 286, box 9.

Book HH: grants for lots held from the 1820, 1821, and 1827 land lotteries. Georgia Archives microfilm, drawer 286, box 40.

Book "Square or Fractional Lots, 1850": grants for square and fractional lots suspended from a public sale in December 1847. Index entries referencing this book are written "Frac 1850." Georgia Archives microfilm, drawer 286, box 10.

Forfeited Land Grant Book

Forfeited Land. Most grants are for land in original Appling County. Georgia Archives microfilm, drawer 286, box 39.

Fraudulent Draws Grant Books

All four fraudulent draw grant books are located in Georgia Archives microfilm, drawer 286, box 10.

Fraudulent Reverted Land, Book A
Fraudulent Draws, Book B (1820, 1821, and 1827 lotteries)
Fraudulent Draws, Book B (1821 and 1827 lotteries)
1832 Cherokee Fraudulent Lots

Relinquished Lots Grant Book

Relinquished Lots. Grants for undrawn lots and lots relinquished to the state. Georgia Archives microfilm, drawer 286, box 39.

Miscellaneous Lots Grant Book

Miscellaneous. Grants for various lots across all land lotteries. Georgia Archives microfilm, drawer 286, box 10.

Plats and Maps

Identifying the land on historic and modern maps is an important part of researching the history of a land lot. Four map resources fulfill the needs of most researchers. These include: individual plats, district plats, county land lot maps, and county tax parcel maps. The first three are available at the Georgia Archives and, for the majority of counties, the current tax parcel maps can be accessed online.

Individual Plats

Land lot plats are recorded in books arranged geographically by county, district, and land lot. These detailed surveys show boundary stations, watercourses, roads, swamps, and other distinctive features. The following information is recorded with each plat: surveyor, survey date, chain carriers, scale, and magnetic variation. The name of the person who drew the lot is written on the side of the plat. Plat book references for each original county can be found in the land lottery chapters of this book, beginning on page 77. This plat of land in Houston County is on Indian Creek and identifies an old road or trail.

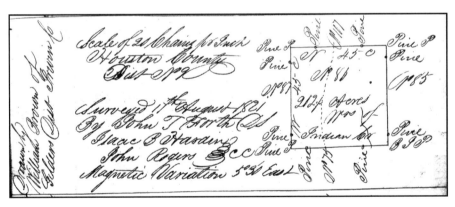

Figure 14. Plat of Houston County, District 9, Land Lot 86

District Plats

Each surveyor produced a district plat, showing the arrangement of land lots in relation to each other. These maps are similar to township plats used in Federal land states, except that the district plats do not include the names of any individual owners. The original district plats are maintained by the Georgia Archives, in Record Group 3-3-24. All of them have been scanned and made available online in Georgia's Virtual Vault, at http://content.sos.state.ga.us/. Go to "District Plats of Survey" and browse for the county and district of interest to view the plat.

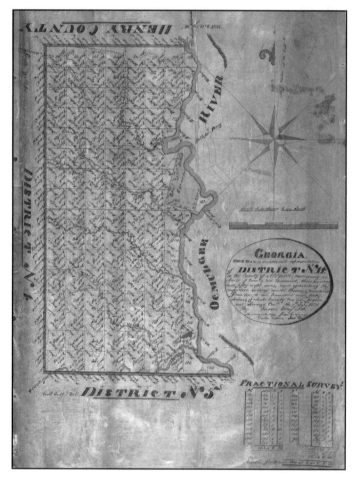

Figure 15. District plat, Monroe County, District 14

County Land Lot Maps

All counties in land lottery areas of Georgia have maps identifying the districts and land lots within their boundaries. Land lot maps available at the Georgia Archives date from the 1860s and can be accessed by requesting the County Map File for the county in question. Maps found in this collection vary widely from county to county; the most common being Georgia Department of Transportation maps. Both historic and modern land lot maps are available for most counties. Early land lot maps dating from the 1860s have been scanned and made available online by the Georgia Archives at http://content.sos.state.ga.us/.

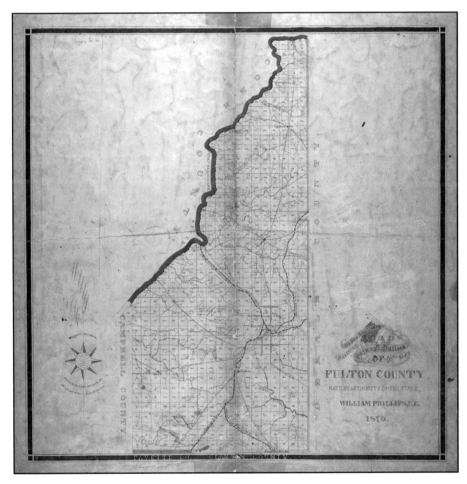

Figure 16. *Map of Fulton County*, by William Phillips, 1870

County Tax Parcel Maps

Map records in the tax assessor's office in land lottery counties almost always reference district and land lot boundaries. Tax parcel maps are detailed depictions of subdivided parcels and provide the specific location of the current boundaries of land lots. Parcel maps can be found in the tax assessor's office in the county where the land is located, a good place to look for countywide land lot maps. The majority of Georgia's counties have put their current tax parcel maps online, although many charge a fee to access the data. To find the county tax assessor website in question, visit www.gaassessors.com.

Figure 17. Pickens County Tax Parcel Map, 2010.
Courtesy Pickens County Tax Assessor.

Records relating to the land lotteries and land lot surveys can be found anywhere that land is described, transacted, and adjudicated: state financial records detail fees paid for grants; titles to land lots can be researched in county deed records; lawsuits over land lot titles can be found in county Superior Court records, state Supreme Court files, and in Federal District Court cases. Both the Legislature and the Executive Department issued clarifications relating to land lots and property law through laws, resolutions, and executive orders. And, newspaper advertisements announced the sale of certain lots of land. The records detailed in this chapter do not apply to every land lot, but are useful for compiling a broader history of each tract of land.

Land Lottery Records

Researchers should always look in the Land Lottery Records files for original documents related to land lots. Organized by land lot, these files contain a wide variety of loose papers related to land lot grants. They may include affidavits, original grants, powers of attorney, certificates, original executive orders, and many miscellaneous documents. A significant selection of these records was abstracted by Robert Scott Davis, Jr., and Silas Emmett Lucas, Jr., in *The Georgia Land Lottery Papers, 1805–1914*. The papers are available in original form at the Georgia Archives in Land Lottery Records, Record Group 3-5-28.

Record numbers included here are for reference purposes but not used in citations.

County	Ga. Archives Record
Appling	DOC-6004
Baldwin, Carroll	DOC-6002
Cherokee, Section 1, Districts 1–4	DOC-6846
Cherokee, Section 1, District 5–10	DOC-6847
Cherokee, Section 1, Districts 11–13S	DOC-6848

County	Ga. Archives Record
Cherokee, Section 1, Districts 14–19	DOC-6849
Cherokee, Section 2, Districts 1–4	DOC-6850
Cherokee, Section 2, Districts 5–14	DOC-6851
Cherokee, Section 2, Districts 15–18	DOC-6852
Cherokee, Section 2, Districts 19–27	DOC-6853
Cherokee, Section 3, Districts 1–3	DOC-6626
Cherokee, Section 3, Districts 4–12	DOC-6627
Cherokee, Section 3, Districts 13–18	DOC-6629
Cherokee, Section 3, Districts 19–20	DOC-6630
Cherokee, Section 3, Districts 21–28	DOC-6003
Cherokee, Section 4, Districts 1–7	DOC-7187
Cherokee, Section 4, Districts 8–19	DOC-6631
Coweta, Dooly	DOC-6632
Early, Fayette, Gwinnett, Habersham, Hall	DOC-6633
Irwin	DOC2-1104
Lee	DOC-6635
Monroe, Muscogee	DOC-6636
Rabun, Troup, Walton, Wayne, Wilkinson	DOC-6637
Unidentified	DOC-6637

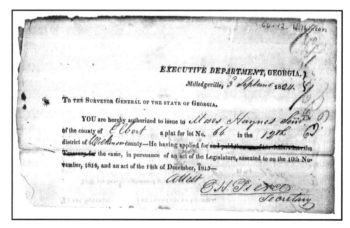

Figure 18. Certificate authorizing a plat to Moses Haynes.

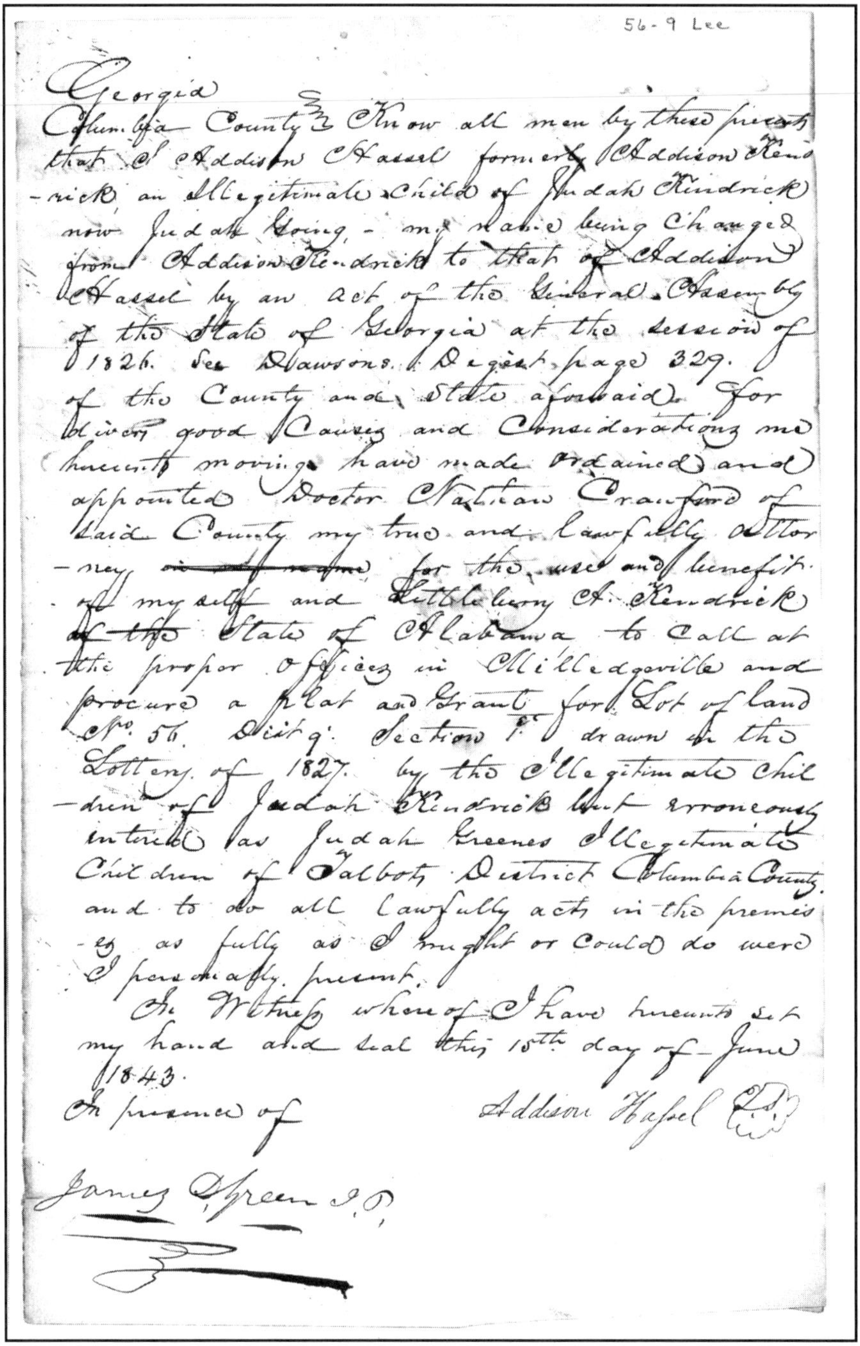

56-9 Lee

Georgia
Columbia County } Know all men by these presents
that I Addison Hassel formerly Addison Kend
-rick, an Illegitimate Child of Judah Kindrick
now Judah Going - my name being Changed
from Addison Kendrick to that of Addison
Hassel by an act of the General Assembly
of the State of Georgia at the session of
1826. See Dawsons Digest page 329.
of the County and State aforesaid for
divers good Causes and Considerations me
hereunto moving have made ordained and
appointed Doctor Nathan Crawford of
said County my true and lawfully Attor
-ney ~~in my name~~ for the use and benefit
of my self and Littleberry A. Kendrick
~~of the~~ State of Alabama to Call at
the proper Offices in Milledgeville and
procure a Plat and Grant for Lot of land
No. 56. Dist 9. Section 1st drawn in the
Lottery of 1827 by the Illegitimate Chil
-dren of Judah Kendrick but erroneously
entered as Judah Greenes Illegitimate
Children of Talbots District Columbia County
and to do all lawfully acts in the premis
-es as fully as I might or could do were
I personally present.
In Witness whereof I have hereunto set
my hand and seal this 15th day of June
1843.

In presence of Addison Hassel (L.S.)

James Green J.P.

Figure 19. Petition of Addison Hassel, identifying himself as the illegitimate child of Judah Going.

Executive Department Minutes

For the lottery years, the Executive Department Minutes contain notations of grants issued, warrants for payment related to the lotteries, and executive orders making corrections to land grants. Copies of executive orders changing information on grants are attached to and filmed with their associated records. The minute books are indexed by name and subject matter. However, clerks were not always consistent about the way particular entries were indexed. Minute books are available on microfilm at the Georgia Archives.

Minute Books	**Ga. Archives Microfilm**
1802–1805, 1805–1806	Drawer 50, Box 45
1806–1808, 1808–1809	Drawer 50, Box 46
1809–1810, 1811–1812, 1812–1814	Drawer 50, Box 47
1814–1815, 1816–1817, 1819–1821	Drawer 50, Box 48
1822–1825, 1825–1827	Drawer 50, Box 49
1829–1832, 1832–1834	Drawer 50, Box 50
1834–1839, 1839–1843	Drawer 50, Box 51
1843–1849, 1849–1855	Drawer 50, Box 52
1855–1859	Drawer 50, Box 53

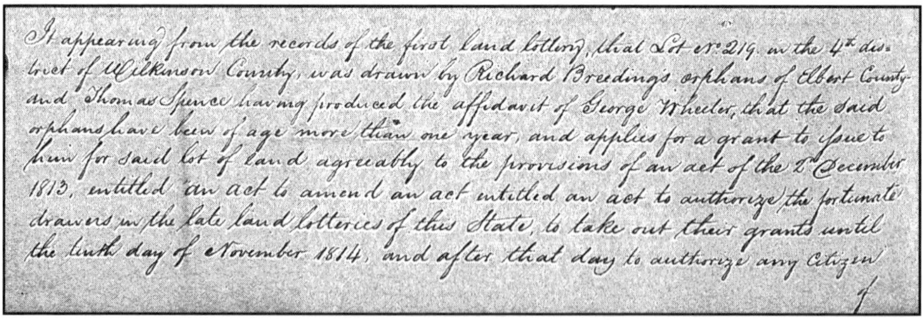
It appearing from the records of the first land lottery, that Lot No. 219 in the 4th district of Wilkinson County, was drawn by Richard Breeding's orphans of Elbert County and Thomas Spence having produced the affidavit of George Wheeler, that the said orphans have been of age more than one year, and applies for a grant to issue to him for said lot of land agreeably to the provisions of an act of the 2d December 1813, entitled "an act to amend an act entitled an act to authorize the fortunate drawers in the late land lotteries of this State, to take out their grants until the tenth day of November 1814, and after that day to authorize any Citizen of

Figure 20. Executive Department Minutes, 23 December 1823, concerning the draw of Richard Breeding's orphans of Elbert County.

Financial Records

Financial records document sales, fees, and rents on land lots. These records are recorded in chronological order and are not indexed. Because many fractional lot grants were never recorded, record of their sale is the only remaining evidence that the state relinquished title. These records have not been microfilmed. The following list includes the title and number for each financial record group related to land lotteries at the Georgia Archives.

Title	Record Group
Whole Lot Fees, All Lotteries	3-2-47
1820 Land Lottery Fees, 1821–1850	3-2-44
Land Lottery Fraction Sales, 1805–1806	3-6-30
Fractional Grant Fees, 1821–1859	3-2-46
Fraudulently Drawn Lots Fees, 1824–1855	3-2-49
Grant Fees Paid, 1836–1842	3-2-53
Reverted Lot Sales, 1828–1859	3-2-51
Sales/Forfeited Lots/Fractions/Reserve Lots/Town Lots, 1823–1834	3-2-52
Fractions, Reserves and Whole Lot Sales, Mortgages, 1805–1829	3-2-48
Sale of Lots/Fractions/Islands/Reserves/Forfeited, 1828–1835	3-2-50

Courts

Lawsuits over land lots can be found in local, state, and federal court records. Because of the complexity of these records, they are not described in detail here. At the local level, cases concerning land are heard in Superior Court. Georgia did not have an appellate court until the Georgia Supreme Court heard its first case in January 1846. Superior Court and Supreme Court case files are available at the Georgia Archives, both on microfilm. Relevant district court records are available at the National Archives Southeast Region.

Laws and Resolutions

Besides the land lottery authorization acts, many personal laws were used to address particular legal issues encountered by individuals. Both the House and Senate passed resolutions addressing problems related to land lottery administration (Figure 21). Georgia laws are available at the Georgia Archives and most years have been made available online. To locate legislative action, search for names and land lot numbers. The most useful search is a proximity search.

Georgia Legislative Documents
http://www.galileo.usg.edu/express?link=zlgl

Laws were also published in digests at regular intervals. The two most useful digests of Georgia laws for land lottery research are those published by Oliver Prince in 1837 and by T. R. R. Cobb in 1851. Both are available at the Georgia Archives or on Google Books at books.google.com.

Digest of the Laws of the State of Georgia, Oliver H. Prince, 1837.

Digest of the Statute Laws of the State of Georgia, T. R. R. Cobb, 1851.

Cities

Land in Milledgeville, Macon, and Columbus was reserved and sold at public auction in processes separate from the land lotteries. Records of the Milledgeville commissioners include the names of individuals who purchased town lots. The minute book is not indexed, but is easy to browse. Grants to town lots in Macon and Columbus are indexed by lot number and name in the grant books.

Milledgeville (Georgia Archives microfilm, drawer 70, box 37)

Executive Department, Board State Commissioners of Milledgeville, 1804–1812 (Journal)

Macon (Georgia Archives microfilm, drawer 286, box 41.)

Town Lots, 1824–1851
Town Lots, 1829–1849
Macon Reserve, 1829–1850
Macon Reserve, 1829–1859

Columbus (Georgia Archives microfilm, drawer 286, boxes 41-42)

Town Lot Grants, 1830-1851

Town Lot Grants, 1855-1869

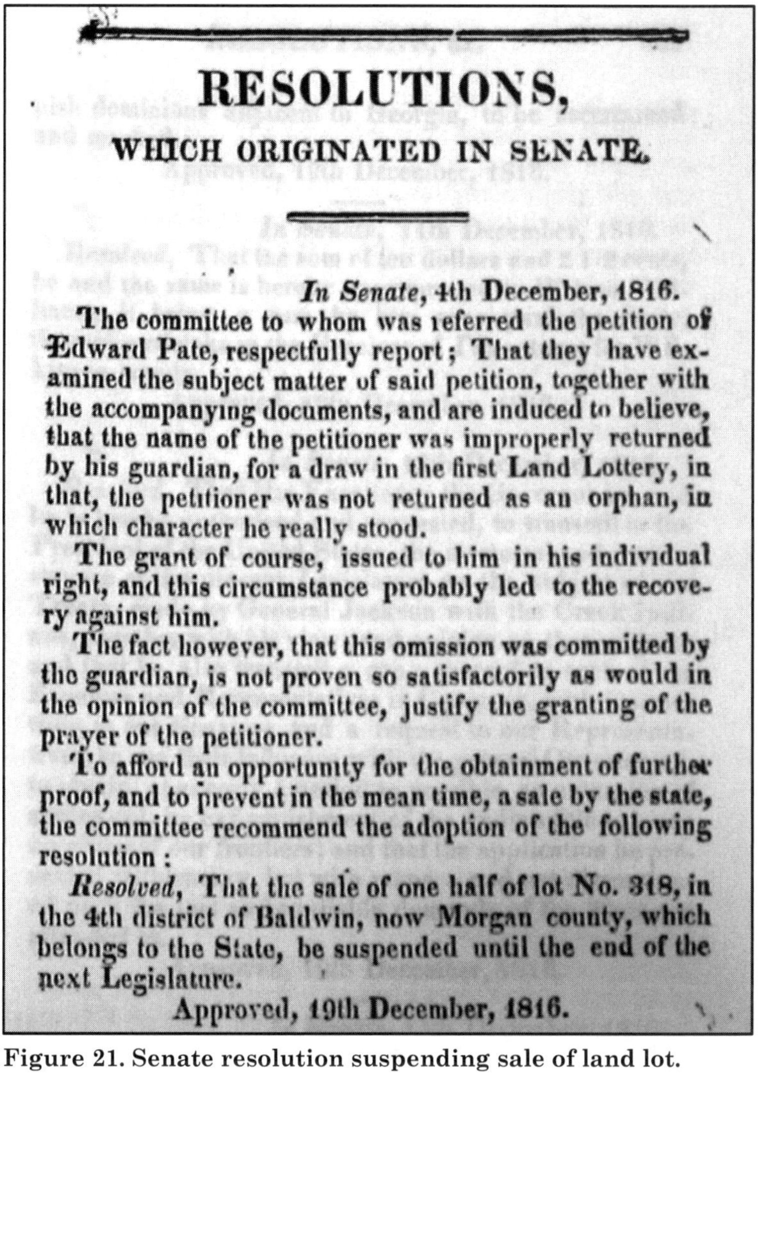

RESOLUTIONS,

WHICH ORIGINATED IN SENATE.

In Senate, 4th December, 1816.

The committee to whom was referred the petition of Edward Pate, respectfully report; That they have examined the subject matter of said petition, together with the accompanying documents, and are induced to believe, that the name of the petitioner was improperly returned by his guardian, for a draw in the first Land Lottery, in that, the petitioner was not returned as an orphan, in which character he really stood.

The grant of course, issued to him in his individual right, and this circumstance probably led to the recovery against him.

The fact however, that this omission was committed by the guardian, is not proven so satisfactorily as would in the opinion of the committee, justify the granting of the prayer of the petitioner.

To afford an opportunity for the obtainment of further proof, and to prevent in the mean time, a sale by the state, the committee recommend the adoption of the following resolution :

Resolved, That the sale of one half of lot No. 318, in the 4th district of Baldwin, now Morgan county, which belongs to the State, be suspended until the end of the next Legislature.

Approved, 19th December, 1816.

Figure 21. Senate resolution suspending sale of land lot.

Reserves

In addition to three cities, eleven small tracts of land were reserved and granted under separate processes from the land lotteries. To learn more about the history and records of the reserves, see Chapter 9 in Farris Cadle's *Georgia Land Surveying History and Law*. See the following pages in this book to find each reserve on a map.

Reserve	Map
Fort Hawkins	86
Creek Indian Agency	118
Indian Springs	112
McIntosh's Lower	112
McIntosh's Upper	124
Buckey Barnard	118
James Barnard	118
Michey Barnard	118
Efau Emathlaw	118
Marshall's Ferry	128

Newspapers

Numerous Georgia newspapers have been digitized and made available online. Newspapers published land lottery news, lists of fortunate drawers, and advertisements for sheriff sales. Later advertisements for land sales often reference land lot and district numbers. Milledgeville, Macon, and Columbus newspapers are the most useful source for information about the land lotteries and individual land lots. Major newspapers from those locations have been scanned and made available at no fee through the Digital Library of Georgia.

Milledgeville: http://milledgeville.galileo.usg.edu/milledgeville/search
Macon: http://telegraph.galileo.usg.edu/telegraph/search
Columbus: http://enquirer.galileo.usg.edu/enquirer/search

Fraudulent Drawers

Registration for the land lotteries required that participants take an oral oath that they were eligible. For each land lottery, the legislature provided an ingenious method to identify people who gave a false oath. An informant with knowledge that a participant registered under false pretenses could bring a suit in the Superior Court in the county where the registrant lived. If the informant could prove that the registration was invalid, the lot was condemned by the state and divided in half. The informant then received one half and Georgia sold the other half. Records of lots condemned as fraudulently drawn can be found in Georgia Archives Record Group 3-6-32. They are also abstracted in Chapter 3, "Liars," in *The Georgia Black Book*, by Robert Scott Davis, Jr.

1805 Georgia Land Lottery

Treaty	16 June 1802, Fort Wilkinson
Law	11 May 1803
Lot Sizes	202.5 acres: Baldwin, Wilkinson
	490 acres in Wayne
Lot Orientation	45 degrees: Baldwin, Wilkinson
	13 degrees / 77 degrees: Wayne
Registration	11 May 1803 – 1 March 1804
Drawing	22 July 1805 – 31 August 1805
Fractions Sale	27 August 1806 – 31 October 1806
Reverted Lots	Sold beginning 10 January 1816
First Counties	Baldwin, Wilkinson, Wayne

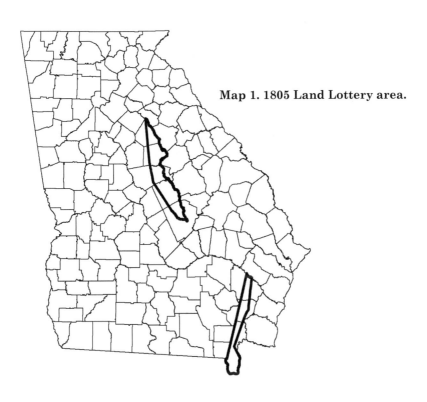

Map 1. 1805 Land Lottery area.

Original Baldwin County Map

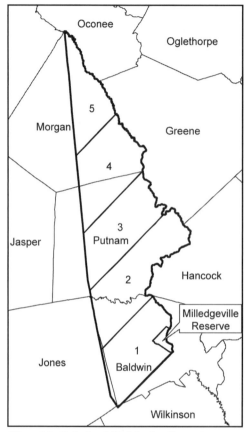

Map 16. Original Baldwin County.

Original Baldwin County Records

Plats

Districts	Georgia Archives Microfilm
1–5	Drawer 51, Box 35

Grants

Book	Georgia Archives Microfilm
Districts 1–4	Drawer 53, Box 15
District 5	Drawer 53, Box 16
Reverted, Book A	Drawer 286, Box 11
Reverted, Book B	Drawer 286, Box 12

Land Lot Size and Orientation, Baldwin

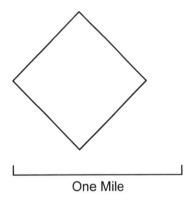

Area: 202.5 acres
Side: 45 chains or 2,970 feet
Bearing: 45 degrees east from north

One Mile

Original Wilkinson County Map

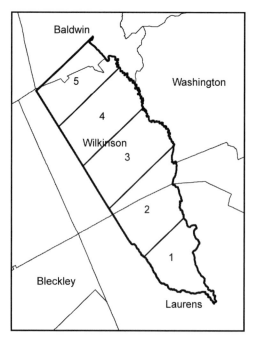

Map 17. Original Wilkinson County.

Original Wilkinson County Records

Plats

Districts

1–5

Georgia Archives Microfilm

Drawer 51, Box 35

Grants

Book

District 1

Districts 2–5

Reverted A

Reverted B

Georgia Archives Microfilm

Drawer 285, Box 101

Drawer 285, Box 102

Drawer 286, Box 11

Drawer 286, Box 12

Land Lot Size and Orientation, Wilkinson

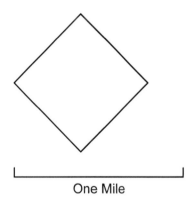

One Mile

Area: 202.5 acres
Side: 45 chains or 2,970 feet
Bearing: 45 degrees east from north

Original Wayne County Map

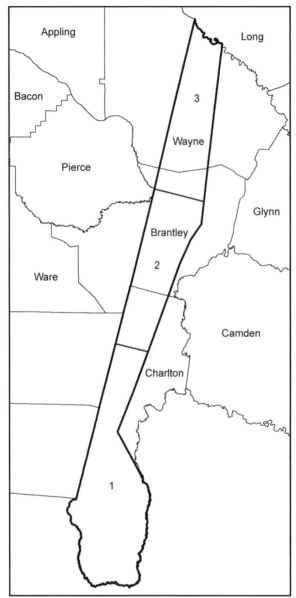

Map 18. Original Wayne County

Original Wayne County Records

Plats

Districts	*Georgia Archives Microfilm*
1–3	Drawer 51, Box 36

Grants

Book	*Georgia Archives Microfilm*
Districts 1–3	Drawer 285, Box 101
Reverted	Drawer 285, Box 101

Land Lot Size and Orientation, Wayne

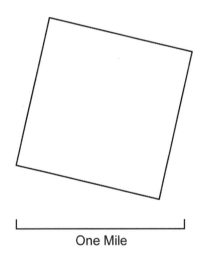

Area: 490 acres
Side: 70 chains or 4,620 feet
Bearing: 13 degrees east from north

One Mile

Qualifications, 1805 Land Lottery

Requirements	Draws
Free white male, age 21 or older, 1 year residence in Georgia (or paid tax to state), U.S. citizen	One
Free white male, age 21 or older, 1 year residence in Georgia (or paid tax to state), U.S. citizen, with wife and/or legitimate children	Two
Widow, with child under age 21, 1 year residence in Georgia	Two
Orphan or orphan family, under age 21, with parents dead, or father dead and mother remarried.	One

1807 Georgia Land Lottery

Treaty	14 Nov 1805, Washington City
Law	26 June 1806
Lot Size	202.5 acres
Lot Orientation	45 degrees
Registration	26 June 1806 – 26 September 1806
Drawing	10 August 1807 – 23 September 1807
Fractions Sale	1 December 1807 – 26 February 1808
Reverted Lots	Sold beginning 10 January 1816
First Counties	Baldwin and Wilkinson addition

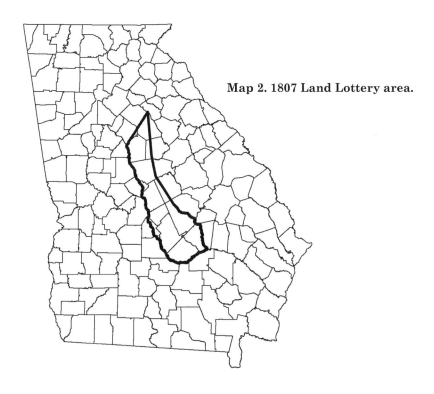

Map 2. 1807 Land Lottery area.

Original Baldwin County (Extension) Map

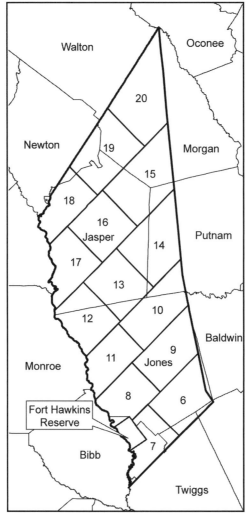

Map 20. Original Baldwin County Extension.

Original Baldwin County (Extension) Records

Plats

Districts	*Georgia Archives Microfilm*
6	Drawer 51, Box 37
7	Drawer 51, Box 36
8–11	Drawer 51, Box 37
12 (lots 1–88)	Drawer 51, Box 38
12 (lots 89–233)	Drawer 51, Box 36
13–14	Drawer 51, Box 38
15	Drawer 51, Box 37
16–17	Drawer 51, Box 36
18	Drawer 51, Box 37
19–20	Drawer 51, Box 38

Grants

Book	*Georgia Archives Microfilm*
Districts 6–9	Drawer 53, Box 16
Districts 10–14	Drawer 53, Box 17
Districts 15–20	Drawer 53, Box 18
Reverted, Book B	Drawer 286, Box 12

Land Lot Size and Orientation, Baldwin

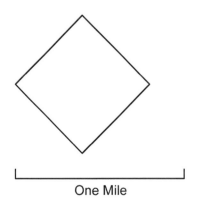

Area: 202.5 acres
Side: 45 chains or 2,970 feet
Bearing: 45 degrees east from north

One Mile

Original Wilkinson County (Extension) Map

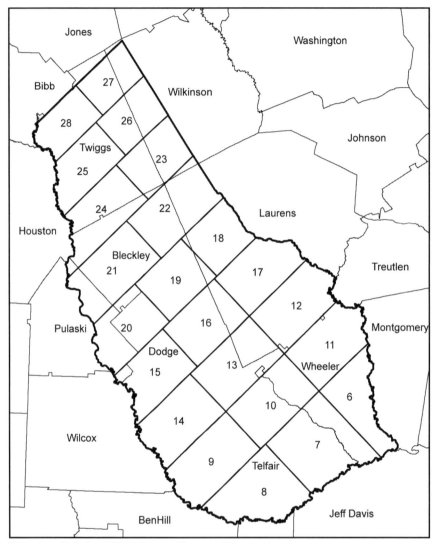

Map 21. Original Wilkinson County Extension.

Original Wilkinson County (Extension) Records

Plats

Districts	Georgia Archives Microfilm
6–8	Drawer 51, Box 38
9	Drawer 51, Box 36
10	Drawer 51, Box 37
11–12	Drawer 51, Box 38
13	Drawer 51, Box 36
14	Drawer 51, Box 38
15–16	Drawer 51, Box 36
17	Drawer 51, Box 37
18–21	Drawer 51, Box 36
22–24	Drawer 51, Box 38
25	Drawer 51, Box 37
26	Drawer 51, Box 38
27	Drawer 51, Box 36
28 (lots 1–204)	Drawer 51, Box 38
28 (lots 205–236)	Drawer 51, Box 37

Grants

Book	Georgia Archives Microfilm
Districts 6–13	Drawer 285, Box 103
Districts 14–21	Drawer 285, Box 104
Districts 22–25	Drawer 286, Box 1
Districts 26–28	Drawer 286, Box 2
Reverted, Book B	Drawer 286, Box 12
Reverted, Book C	Drawer 286, Box 13

Land Lot Size and Orientation, Wilkinson

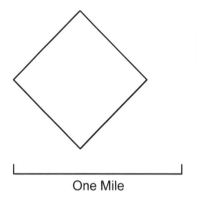

Area: 202.5 acres
Side: 45 chains or 2,970 feet
Bearing: 45 degrees east from north

One Mile

Qualifications, 1807 Land Lottery

Requirements (everyone)

U.S. citizen

3 years residence in Georgia

Requirements	Draws
Free white male, age 21 or older	One
Free white male, age 21 or older, with wife and/or legitimate children	Two
Widow	One
Free white female, unmarried, age 21 or older	One
Family of orphans, under age 21, father dead	One
Orphan family, under age 21, with both parents dead, or father dead and mother remarried.	Two
Orphan, under age 21, with both parents dead	One

Excluded

Winners in previous land lottery

1820 Georgia Land Lottery

Treaties	9 Aug 1814, Fort Jackson
	8 July 1817, Cherokee Agency
	22 January 1818, Creek Agency, Flint River
Laws	15 December 1818, 16 December 1819
Lot Sizes	490 acres, Irwin, Appling; 250 acres, other counties
Lot Orientation	0 degrees / 90 degrees: Early, Irwin, Appling, Hall, Habersham, Rabun; 60 degrees / 30 degrees: Gwinnett, Walton, Hall, Habersham
Registration	15 December 1818 – 15 March 1819
	13 December 1819 – 31 May 1820
Drawing	1 September 1820 – 2 December 1820
Fractions Sale	6 August 1821 – 31 August 1821
Reverted Lots	Sold beginning 1 September 1841
First Counties	Early, Irwin, Appling, Rabun, Habersham, Hall, Gwinnett, Walton

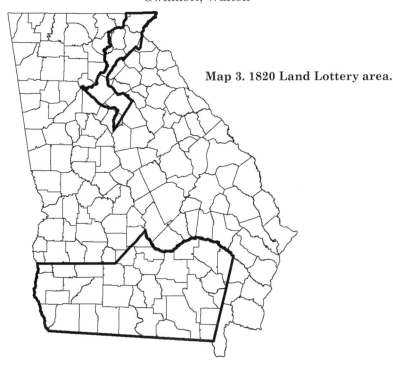

Map 3. 1820 Land Lottery area.

Original Early County Map

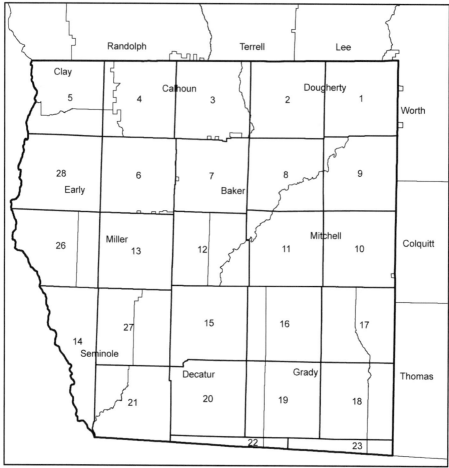

Map 23. Original Early County.

Original Early County Records

Plats

Districts	Georgia Archives Microfilm
1–9	Drawer 51, Box 39
9–21	Drawer 51, Box 40
21–28	Drawer 51, Box 41
Reverted	Drawer 51, Box 41

Grants

Book	Georgia Archives Microfilm
Districts 1–2	Drawer 54, Box 17
Districts 3–6	Drawer 54, Box 18
Districts 7–10	Drawer 54, Box 19
Districts 11–14	Drawer 54, Box 20
Districts 15–18	Drawer 54, Box 21
Districts 19–22	Drawer 54, Box 22
Districts 23, 26–28	Drawer 54, Box 23
Supplement, Book A	Drawer 54, Box 23
Supplement, Book B	Drawer 54, Box 24
Reverted, Books A and B	Drawer 54, Box 24
Reverted, Books C and D	Drawer 54, Box 25

Land Lot Size and Orientation, Early

Area: 250 acres
Side: 50 chains or 3,300 feet
Bearing: north

One Mile

Original Irwin County Map

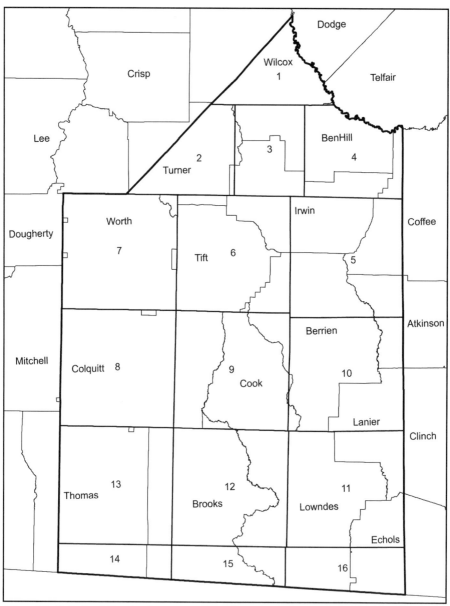

Map 24. Original Irwin County.

Original Irwin County Records

Plats

Districts	*Georgia Archives Microfilm*
1–13	Drawer 51, Box 42
14 (lots 1–135, 138, 149)	Drawer 51, Box 42
14 (lots 136, 137, 139–179)	Drawer 51, Box 43
15–16	Drawer 51, Box 43
Reverted	Drawer 51, Box 43

Grants

Book	*Georgia Archives Microfilm*
Districts 1–5	Drawer 285, Box 75
Districts 6–9	Drawer 285, Box 76
Districts 10–12	Drawer 285, Box 77
Districts 13–16	Drawer 285, Box 78
Supplement	Drawer 285, Box 78
Reverted, Books A and B	Drawer 285, Box 79
Reverted, Book C (1841)	Drawer 285, Box 80
Reverted, Book D (1841)	Drawer 285, Box 36
Irwin 1840	Drawer 285, Box 80

Land Lot Size and Orientation, Irwin

Area: 490 acres
Side: 70 chains or 4,620 feet
Bearing: north

One Mile

Original Appling County Map

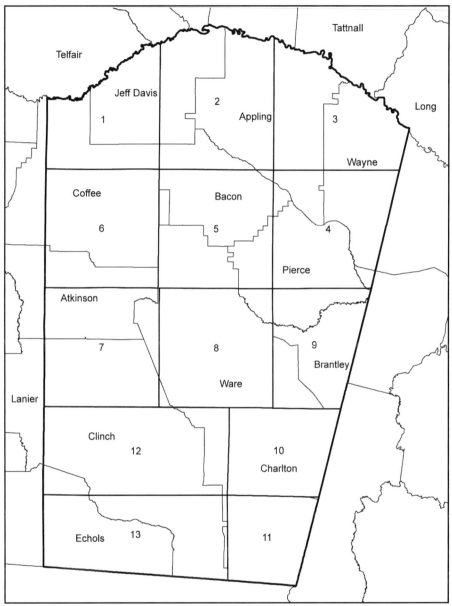

Map 25. Original Appling County.

Original Appling County Records

Plats

Districts	Georgia Archives Microfilm
1–3	Drawer 51, Box 43
4	Drawer 51, Box 43
4	Drawer 51, Box 44
5–7	Drawer 51, Box 44
7–9	Drawer 51, Box 44
10–11	Drawer 51, Box 45
12–13	Drawer 51, Box 44
12–13	Drawer 51, Box 45
Reverted	Drawer 51, Box 45

Grants

Book	Georgia Archives Microfilm
District 1	Drawer 53, Box 9
Districts 2–5	Drawer 53, Box 10
Districts 6–11	Drawer 53, Box 11
Districts 12–13	Drawer 53, Box 12
Districts 12–13, Vol. 2	Drawer 53, Box 12
Supplement	Drawer 53, Box 12
Reverted, Books A and B	Drawer 53, Box 13
Reverted, Books C and D	Drawer 53, Box 14

Land Lot Size and Orientation, Appling

Area: 490 acres
Side: 70 chains or 4,620 feet
Bearing: north

One Mile

Original Walton County Map

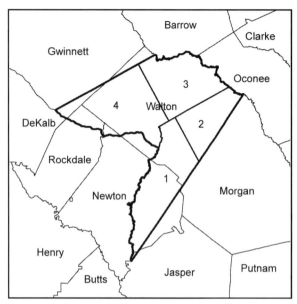

Map 26. Original Walton County.

Original Walton County Records

Plats

Districts	*Georgia Archives Microfilm*
1–3	Drawer 51, Box 44
4 (lots 1–160)	Drawer 51, Box 44
4 (lots 161–351)	Drawer 51, Box 46

Grants

Book	*Georgia Archives Microfilm*
Districts 1–4	Drawer 285, Box 100
Supplement	Drawer 286, Box 3

Land Lot Size and Orientation, Walton

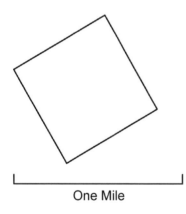

Area: 250 acres
Side: 50 chains or 3,300 feet
Bearing: 60 degrees east of north

One Mile

Original Gwinnett County Map

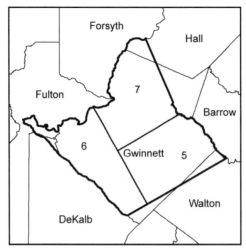

Map 27. Original Gwinnett County.

Original Gwinnett County Records

Plats

Districts	*Georgia Archives Microfilm*
5–7	Drawer 51, Box 46

Grants

Book	*Georgia Archives Microfilm*
District 5	Drawer 54, Box 26
Districts 6–7	Drawer 54, Box 27
Supplementary	Drawer 286, Box 3

Land Lot Size and Orientation, Gwinnett

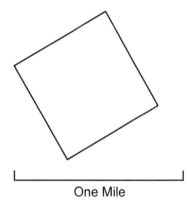

Area: 250 acres
Side: 50 chains or 3,300 feet
Bearing: 60 degrees east of north

One Mile

Original Hall County Map

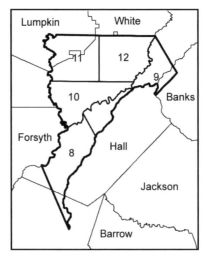

Map 28. Original Hall County.

Original Hall County Records

Plats

Districts
8–12

Georgia Archives Microfilm
Drawer 51, Box 46

Grants

Book
Districts 8–12
Reverted, Book D (1841)
Supplement

Georgia Archives Microfilm
Drawer 54, Box 29
Drawer 286, Box 36
Drawer 286, Box 3

Land Lot Size and Orientation, Hall

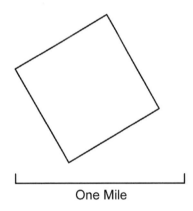

Area: 250 acres
Side: 50 chains or 3,300 feet
Bearing: 60 degrees east of north
Districts: 8, 9

One Mile

Area: 250 acres
Side: 50 chains or 3,300 feet
Bearing: north
Districts: 10, 11, 12

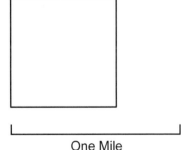

One Mile

Original Habersham County Map

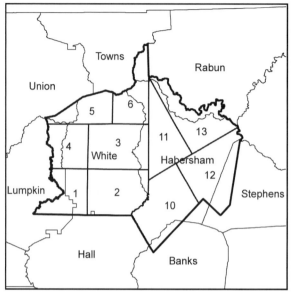

Map 29. Original Habersham County.

Original Habersham County Records

Plats

Districts	*Georgia Archives Microfilm*
1–6, 10–13	Drawer 51, Box 46

Grants

Book	*Georgia Archives Microfilm*
Districts 1–4	Drawer 54, Box 27
Districts 5–6, 10–13	Drawer 54, Box 28
Reverted, Book D (1841)	Drawer 286, Box 36
Supplement	Drawer 286, Box 3

Land Lot Size and Orientation, Habersham

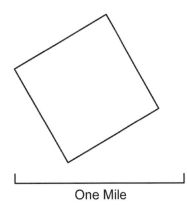

Area: 250 acres
Side: 50 chains or 3,300 feet
Bearing: 60 degrees east of north
Districts: 10, 11, 12, 13

One Mile

Area: 250 acres
Side: 50 chains or 3,300 feet
Bearing: north
Districts: 1, 2, 3, 4, 5, 6

One Mile

Original Rabun County Map

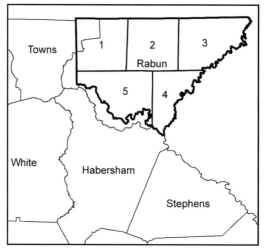

Map 30. Original Rabun County.

Original Rabun County Records

Plats

Districts	*Georgia Archives Microfilm*
1–5	Drawer 51, Box 46

Grants

Book	*Georgia Archives Microfilm*
Districts 1–5	Drawer 285, Box 97
District 2, Book B	Drawer 285, Box 97
Reverted, Book D (1841)	Drawer 286, Box 36
Supplement	Drawer 286, Box 3

Land Lot Size and Orientation, Rabun

Area: 250 acres
Side: 50 chains or 3,300 feet
Bearing: north

One Mile

Qualifications, 1820 Land Lottery

Requirements (everyone)

U.S. citizen

3 years residence in Georgia, or soldier in the "late Indian war"

Requirements	Draws
White male, age 18 or older	One
White male, age 18 or older, with wife and/or legitimate son under age 18, or unmarried daughter	Two
Widow	One
Family of orphans, under age 21, father dead, except those entitled to draw under other requirements	One
Family of orphans, three or more, both parents dead	Two
Family of orphans, one or two, both parents dead	One
Indigent or invalid veteran of Revolutionary War or War of 1812	Two
Veteran of Indian War	One

Additional Draws

Indigent or invalid veteran of Revolutionary War or War of 1812 who was a fortunate drawer in previous lottery	One
Widow or family of orphans, husband or father killed in the Indian Wars or War of 1812	One

Excluded

Winners in previous land lottery, except families of orphans made up of more than one person and those eligible for additional draws

Citizens legally drafted in the War of 1812 who refused to serve or hire a substitute

Those residing in lottery territory prior to treaty

1821 Georgia Land Lottery

Treaty	8 January 1821, Indian Springs
Law	16 May 1821
Lot Size	202.5 acres
Lot Orientation	0 degrees / 90 degrees
Registration	Within two months after 16 May 1821
Drawing	7 November 1821 – 12 December 1821
Fractions Sale	3 November 1823 – 2 February 1824
Reverted Lots	Sold beginning 1 March 1846
First Counties	Henry, Fayette, Monroe, Houston, Dooly

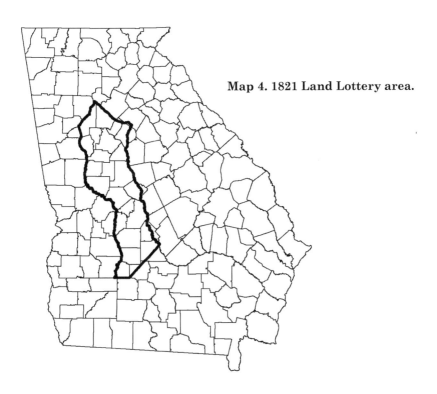

Map 4. 1821 Land Lottery area.

Original Henry County Map

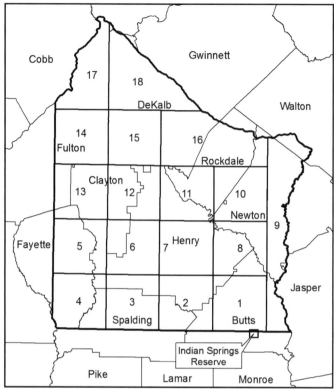

Map 32. Original Henry County.

Original Henry County Records

Plats

Districts	Georgia Archives Microfilm
1–4	Drawer 51, Box 49
5 (lots 1–184)	Drawer 51, Box 49
5 (lots 185–256)	Drawer 51, Box 50
6–17	Drawer 51, Box 50
18 (lots 1–236)	Drawer 51, Box 50
18 (lots 237–340)	Drawer 51, Box 51

Grants

Book	Georgia Archives Microfilm
Districts 1–2	Drawer 54, Box 29
Districts 3–8	Drawer 54, Box 30
Districts 9–12	Drawer 54, Box 31
Districts 13–16	Drawer 285, Box 70
Districts 17–18	Drawer 285, Box 71
Supplement	Drawer 285, Box 71
Reverted, Book A	Drawer 286, Box 38

Land Lot Size and Orientation, Henry

Area: 202.5 acres
Side: 45 chains or 2,970 feet
Bearing: north

One Mile

Original Fayette County Map

Map 33. Original Fayette County.

Original Fayette County Records

Plats

Districts	Georgia Archives Microfilm
6, 7, 9, 14	Drawer 51, Box 51

Grants

Book	Georgia Archives Microfilm
Districts 6, 7, 9, 14	Drawer 54, Box 26
Supplement	Drawer 54, Box 26
Reverted, Book A	Drawer 286, Box 38

Land Lot Size and Orientation, Fayette

Area: 202.5 acres
Side: 45 chains or 2,970 feet
Bearing: north

One Mile

Original Monroe County Map

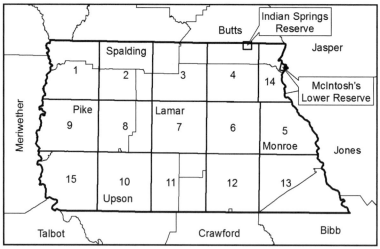

Map 34. Original Monroe County.

Original Monroe County Records

Plats

Districts	Georgia Archives Microfilm
1 (lots 1–84)	Drawer 51, Box 48
1 (lots 85–258)	Drawer 51, Box 49
2–15	Drawer 51, Box 49

Grants

Book	Georgia Archives Microfilm
Districts 1–4	Drawer 285, Box 88
Districts 5–8	Drawer 285, Box 89
Districts 9–12	Drawer 285, Box 90
Districts 13–16	Drawer 285, Box 91
Supplement	Drawer 285, Box 91
Reverted, Book A	Drawer 286, Box 38

Land Lot Size and Orientation, Monroe

Area: 202.5 acres
Side: 45 chains or 2,970 feet
Bearing: north

One Mile

Original Houston County Map

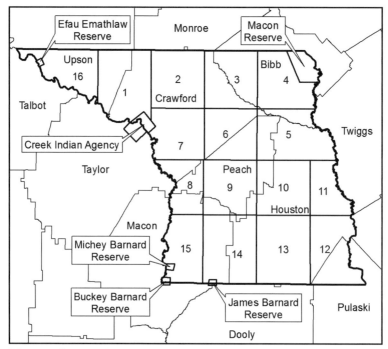

Map 35. Original Houston County.

Original Houston County Records

Plats

Districts	Georgia Archives Microfilm
1	Drawer 51, Box 47
2 (lots 1–220)	Drawer 51, Box 47
2 (lots 221–256)	Drawer 51, Box 48
3–16	Drawer 51, Box 48

Grants

Book	Georgia Archives Microfilm
Districts 1–4	Drawer 285, Box 72
Districts 5–10	Drawer 285, Box 73
Districts 11–14	Drawer 285, Box 74
Districts 15–16	Drawer 285, Box 75
Supplement	Drawer 285, Box 75
Reverted, Book A	Drawer 286, Box 38

Land Lot Size and Orientation, Houston

Area: 202.5 acres
Side: 45 chains or 2,970 feet
Bearing: north

One Mile

Original Dooly County Map

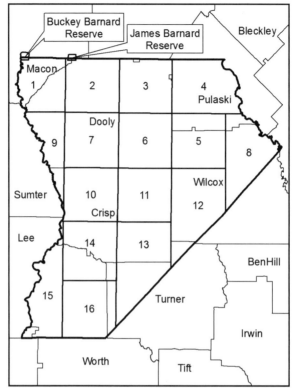

Map 36. Original Dooly County.

Original Dooly County Records

Plats

Districts	Georgia Archives Microfilm
1–4	Drawer 51, Box 46
5 (lots 1–38)	Drawer 51, Box 46
5 (lots 10–253)	Drawer 51, Box 47
6–16	Drawer 51, Box 47
Reverted	Drawer 51, Box 48

Grants

Book	Georgia Archives Microfilm
Districts 1–6	Drawer 54, Box 15
Districts 7–12	Drawer 54, Box 16
Districts 13–16	Drawer 54, Box 17
Supplement	Drawer 54, Box 17
Reverted, Books A and B	Drawer 286, Box 38

Land Lot Size and Orientation, Dooly

Area: 202.5 acres
Side: 45 chains or 2,970 feet
Bearing: north

One Mile

Qualifications, 1821 Land Lottery

Requirements (everyone)

U.S. citizen, 3 years

3 years residence in Georgia

Requirements	Draws
White male, age 18 or older	One
White male, age 18 or older, with wife and/or legitimate son under age 18, or unmarried daughter	Two
Widow	One
Family of orphans, under age 21, father dead, except those entitled to draw under other requirements	One
Family of orphans, three or more, both parents dead	Two
Family of orphans, one or two, both parents dead	One
Children of convict in penitentiary	One

Additional Draws

Widow, husband killed in the Indian Wars or War of 1812	One
Family of orphans, father killed in the Indian Wars or War of 1812	One

Excluded

Winner in previous land lottery

Citizen legally drafted in the War of 1812 who refused to serve or hire a substitute

Deserter

Convict in penitentiary

Individual who left Georgia to escape its laws, had not paid taxes due, or absconded for debt

1827 Georgia Land Lottery

Treaties	12 February 1825, Indian Springs (voided)
	24 January 1826, Washington City
	15 November 1827, Creek Agency
Laws	9 June 1825, 14 and 27 December 1826
Lot Size	202.5 acres
Lot Orientation	0 degrees / 90 degrees
Registration	7 December 1824 – 15 February 1827
Drawing	6 March 1827 –25 May 1827
Fractions Sale	3 November 1828 – 11 March 1829
Reverted Lots	Sold beginning 1 March 1846
First Counties	Carroll, Coweta, Troup, Muscogee, Lee

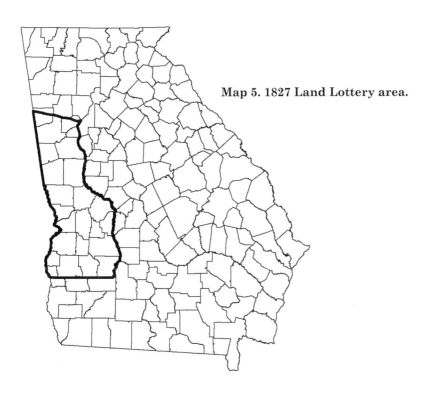

Map 5. 1827 Land Lottery area.

Original Carroll County Map

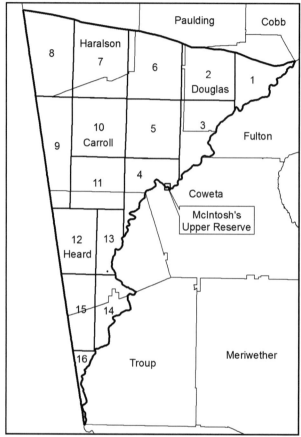

Map 38. Original Carroll County.

Original Carroll County Records

Plats

Districts	Georgia Archives Microfilm
1	Drawer 51, Box 53
2 (lots 1–196)	Drawer 51, Box 53
2 (lots 197–249)	Drawer 51, Box 54
3–9	Drawer 51, Box 54
9–16	Drawer 51, Box 54

Grants

Book	Georgia Archives Microfilm
Districts 1–6	Drawer 53, Box 19
Districts 7–10	Drawer 53, Box 20
Districts 11–16	Drawer 53, Box 21
Reverted	Drawer 286, Box 37
Supplement, Book A	Drawer 286, Box 2

Land Lot Size and Orientation, Carroll

Area: 202.5 acres
Side: 45 chains or 2,970 feet
Bearing: north

One Mile

Original Coweta County Map

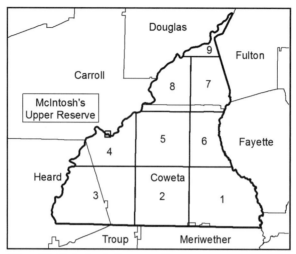

Map 39. Original Coweta County.

Original Coweta County Records

Plats

Districts	Georgia Archives Microfilm
1–4	Drawer 51, Box 51
5 (lots 1–188)	Drawer 51, Box 51
5 (lots 189–256)	Drawer 51, Box 52
6–9	Drawer 51, Box 52

Grants

Book	Georgia Archives Microfilm
Districts 1–2	Drawer 54, Box 13
Districts 3–9	Drawer 54, Box 14
Reverted	Drawer 286, Box 37
Supplementary, Book A	Drawer 286, Box 2

Land Lot Size and Orientation, Coweta

Area: 202.5 acres
Side: 45 chains or 2,970 feet
Bearing: north

One Mile

Original Troup County Map

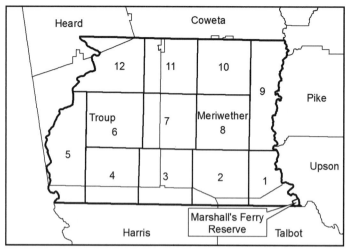

Map 40. Original Troup County.

Original Troup County Records

Plats

Districts	Georgia Archives Microfilm
1–5	Drawer 51, Box 51
6–11	Drawer 51, Box 52
12	Drawer 51, Box 51

Grants

Book	Georgia Archives Microfilm
Districts 1–2	Drawer 285, Box 97
Districts 3–8	Drawer 285, Box 98
Districts 9–12	Drawer 285, Box 99
Reverted	Drawer 287, Box 37
Supplement	Drawer 286, Box 2

Land Lot Size and Orientation, Troup

Area: 202.5 acres
Side: 45 chains or 2,970 feet
Bearing: north

One Mile

Original Muscogee County Map

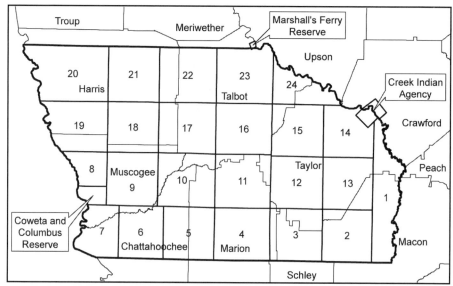

Map 41. Original Muscogee County.

Original Muscogee County Records

Plats

Districts	Georgia Archives Microfilm
1–12	Drawer 51, Box 52
13 (lots 1–68)	Drawer 51, Box 52
13 (lots 69–256)	Drawer 51, Box 53
14–24	Drawer 51, Box 53

Grants

Book	Georgia Archives Microfilm
Districts 1–4	Drawer 285, Box 92
Districts 5–10	Drawer 285, Box 93
Districts 11–16	Drawer 285, Box 94
Districts 17–20	Drawer 285, Box 95
Districts 21–24	Drawer 285, Box 96
Reverted	Drawer 286, Box 37
Reverted, Book B	Drawer 286, Box 38
Supplement, Book A	Drawer 286, Box 2
Supplement, Book B	Drawer 286, Box 3

Land Lot Size and Orientation, Muscogee

Area: 202.5 acres
Side: 45 chains or 2,970 feet
Bearing: north

One Mile

Original Lee County Map

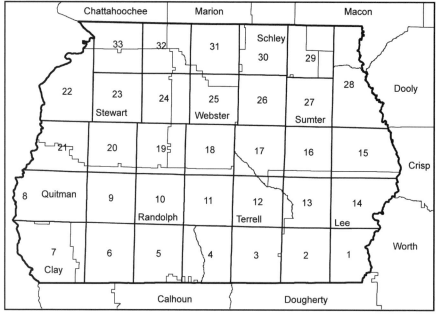

Map 42. Original Lee County.

Original Lee County Records

Plats

Districts	Georgia Archives Microfilm
1	Drawer 51, Box 54
2 (lots 1–152)	Drawer 51, Box 54
2 (lots 43, 130, 153–288)	Drawer 51, Box 55
3–20	Drawer 51, Box 55
21 (lots 1–104, 106, 107)	Drawer 51, Box 55
21 (lots 105, 108–290)	Drawer 51, Box 56
22–33	Drawer 51, Box 56

Grants

Book	Georgia Archives Microfilm
Districts 1–6	Drawer 285, Box 81
Districts 7–10	Drawer 285, Box 82
Districts 11–14	Drawer 285, Box 83
Districts 15–18	Drawer 285, Box 84
Districts 19–22	Drawer 285, Box 85
Districts 23–27	Drawer 285, Box 86
Districts 28–33	Drawer 285, Box 87
Supplement, Book A	Drawer 286, Box 2
Supplement, Book B	Drawer 286, Box 3
Reverted	Drawer 286, Box 37

Land Lot Size and Orientation, Lee

Area: 202.5 acres
Side: 45 chains or 2,970 feet
Bearing: north

One Mile

Qualifications, 1827 Land Lottery

Requirements (everyone)

U.S. citizen, 3 years

3 years residence in Georgia

Requirements	Draws
White male, age 18 or older	One
White male, age 18 or older, with wife and/or legitimate son under age 18, or unmarried daughter	Two
Widow	One
Family of orphans, under age 18, father dead, except those entitled to draw under other requirements	One
Family of orphans, under age 18, three or more [both parents dead]	Two
Family of orphans, under age 18, one or two [both parents dead]	One
Male or unmarried female, age 10 to 18, idiot, insane, lunatic, deaf, dumb, or blind	One
Children of convict in penitentiary treated as orphans	
Illegitimate children, treated as orphans	
Wife and children of man absent from state for three years, treated as widow and orphans	

Additional Draws

	Draws
Widow, husband killed in Revolutionary War, War of 1812, or Indian Wars	One
Family of orphans, father killed in Revolutionary War, War of 1812, or Indian Wars	One
Soldier disabled in Revolutionary War, War of 1812, or Indian Wars	One
Revolutionary War veteran who had not previously won	Two
Revolutionary War veteran who previously won	One
Widow of Revolutionary War veteran	One
Previously won as orphan but now registered as adult	One
Previously won as orphan family, those under age 18	One

Additional Draws

War of 1812 veteran   One

Excluded

Winner in previous land lottery

Citizen legally drafted in the War of 1812 who refused
to serve or hire a substitute

Deserter

Convict in penitentiary

Individual who left Georgia to escape its laws, had not
paid taxes due, or absconded for debt

1832 Georgia Land Lottery

Treaty	14 March 1835, Washington City (not ratified)
	29 December 1835, New Echota
Law	21 December 1830, 24 December 1831
Lot Size	160 acres
Lot Orientation	0 degrees / 90 degrees
Registration	Within four months after 20 February 1832
Drawing	22 October 1832 – 18 February 1833
Reverted Lots	Sold beginning 1 March 1846
First County	Cherokee (Four Sections)

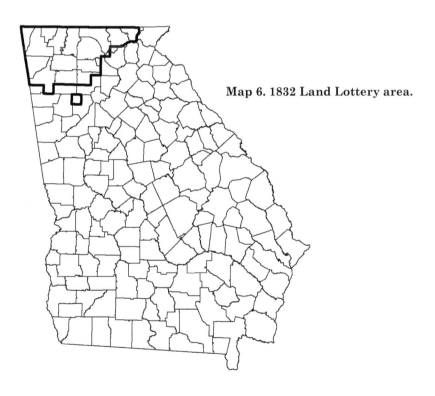

Map 6. 1832 Land Lottery area.

Original Cherokee County, Land Lottery Map
Section One

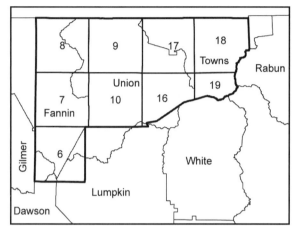

Map 44. Original Cherokee County, Section One, Land Lottery.

Original Cherokee County, Land Lottery Records
Section One

Plats

Districts	*Georgia Archives Microfilm*
6–9	Drawer 51, Box 58
10	Drawer 51, Box 60
16–19	Drawer 51, Box 60

Grants

Book	*Georgia Archives Microfilm*
Districts 6–8	Drawer 53, Box 26
Districts 9–10	Drawer 53, Box 27
Districts 16–17	Drawer 53, Box 31
Districts 18–19	Drawer 53, Box 32

Land Lot Size and Orientation, Cherokee Land Lottery

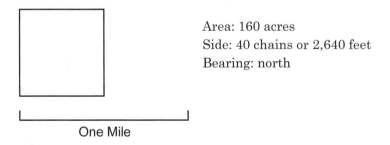

Area: 160 acres
Side: 40 chains or 2,640 feet
Bearing: north

One Mile

Original Cherokee County, Land Lottery Map
Section Two

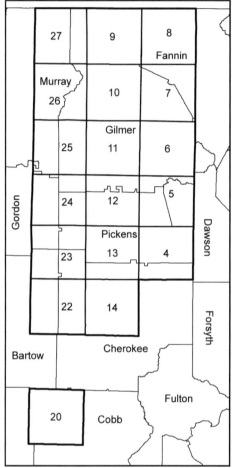

Map 45. Original Cherokee County, Section Two, Land Lottery.

Original Cherokee County, Land Lottery Records
Section Two

Plats

Districts	*Georgia Archives Microfilm*
4–6	Drawer 51, Box 2
8–14	Drawer 51, Box 3
20	Drawer 51, Box 3
22–27	Drawer 51, Box 6

Grants

Book	*Georgia Archives Microfilm*
Districts 4–7	Drawer 53, Box 35
Districts 8–11	Drawer 53, Box 36
Districts 12–14	Drawer 53, Box 37
District 20	Drawer 53, Box 37
Districts 22–23	Drawer 53, Box 43
Districts 24–27	Drawer 53, Box 44

Land Lot Size and Orientation, Cherokee Land Lottery

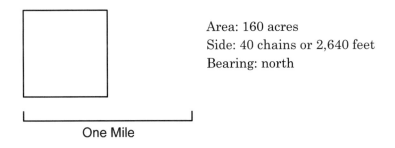

Area: 160 acres
Side: 40 chains or 2,640 feet
Bearing: north

One Mile

Original Cherokee County, Land Lottery Map
Section Three

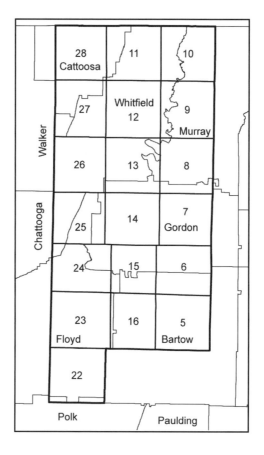

Map 46. Original Cherokee County, Section Three, Land Lottery.

Original Cherokee County, Land Lottery Records
Section Three

Plats

Districts	Georgia Archives Microfilm
5–16	Drawer 51, Box 8
22–28	Drawer 51, Box 11

Grants

Book	Georgia Archives Microfilm
Districts 5–6	Drawer 53, Box 48
Districts 7–10	Drawer 53, Box 49
Districts 11–14	Drawer 53, Box 50
Districts 15–16	Drawer 53, Box 51
Districts 22–25	Drawer 53, Box 56
Districts 26–28	Drawer 53, Box 57

Land Lot Size and Orientation, Cherokee Land Lottery

Area: 160 acres
Side: 40 chains or 2,640 feet
Bearing: north

One Mile

Original Cherokee County, Land Lottery Map
Section Four

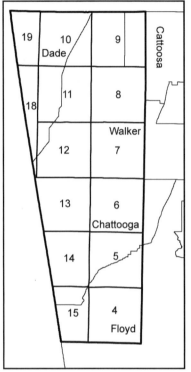

Map 47. Original Cherokee County, Section Four, Land Lottery.

Original Cherokee County, Land Lottery Records
Section Four

Plats

Districts	Georgia Archives Microfilm
4–7	Drawer 51, Box 12
8–15	Drawer 51, Box 13
18–19	Drawer 51, Box 13

Grants

Book	Georgia Archives Microfilm
Districts 5–7	Drawer 53, Box 60
Districts 8–11	Drawer 54, Box 1
Districts 12–15	Drawer 54, Box 2
Districts 18–19	Drawer 54, Box 3

Land Lot Size and Orientation, Cherokee Land Lottery

Area: 160 acres
Side: 40 chains or 2,640 feet
Bearing: north

One Mile

Qualifications, 1832 Land Lottery

Requirements (everyone)

U.S. citizen, 3 years

3 years residence in Georgia

Requirements	Draws
White male, age 18 or older	One
White male, age 18 or older, with wife and/or legitimate son under age 18, or unmarried daughter	Two
Widow	One
Family of orphans, under age 18, [father dead,] except those entitled to draw under other requirements	One
Family of orphans, three or more [both parents dead]	Two
Family of orphans one or two [both parents dead]	One
Deaf, dumb, or blind, not winning previously, and not registered as orphan under separate provision	One
Unmarried female, age 18 or older father died in Revolutionary War, War of 1812, or Indian wars	One
Children of convict in penitentiary treated as orphans	
Illegitimate children, treated as orphans	
Wife and children of man absent from state for three years, treated as widow and orphans	

Additional Draws

	Draws
Widow, husband killed in Revolutionary War, War of 1812, or Indian Wars	One
Family of orphans, father killed in Revolutionary War, War of 1812, or Indian Wars	One
Revolutionary War veteran who had not previously won	Two
Widow of Revolutionary War veteran	One
War of 1812 veteran	One
Veteran of Indian wars from 1784 to 1797	One
Widow of veteran of Indian wars from 1784 to 1797	One
Orphans of veteran of Indian wars from 1784 to 1797	One
Previously won as orphan but now registered as adult	One

Additional Draws

Previously won as orphan family, those under age 18   One

Excluded

Winner in previous land lottery

Those whose family did not meet residency requirements, excepting officers of the U.S. Army or Navy

Citizen legally drafted in the War of 1812 who refused to serve or hire a substitute

Anyone "directly or indirectly concerned" with the Pony Club (gang of thieves)

Convicted felon

Convict in penitentiary

Individual who left Georgia to escape its laws

Mining gold in Cherokee Territory from 1 January 1830

Living in Cherokee Territory

1832 Georgia Gold Lottery

Treaty	14 March 1835, Washington City (not ratified)
	29 December 1835, New Echota
Law	24 December 1831
Lot Size	40 acres
Lot Orientation	0 degrees / 90 degrees
Registration	Within four months after 20 February 1832
Drawing	23 October 1832 – 1 May 1833
Reverted Lots	Sold beginning 1 March 1846
First County	Cherokee

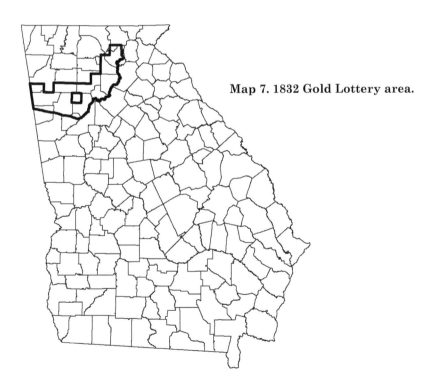

Map 7. 1832 Gold Lottery area.

Original Cherokee County, Gold Lottery Map
Section One

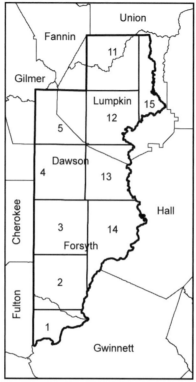

Map 49. Original Cherokee County, Section One, Gold Lottery.

Land Lot Size and Orientation, Cherokee Gold Lottery

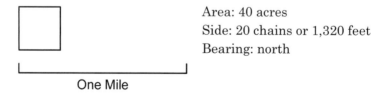

Area: 40 acres
Side: 20 chains or 1,320 feet
Bearing: north

One Mile

Original Cherokee County, Gold Lottery Records
Section One

Plats

Districts	Georgia Archives Microfilm
1	Drawer 51, Box 56
2–4	Drawer 51, Box 57
5	Drawer 51, Box 58
11–12	Drawer 51, Box 59
13 North, 13 South	Drawer 51, Box 59
14–15	Drawer 51, Box 60

Grants

Book	Georgia Archives Microfilm
District 1	Drawer 53, Box 22
District 2, Vol. 1	Drawer 53, Box 22
District 2, Vol. 2	Drawer 53, Box 23
District 3, Vol. 1	Drawer 53, Box 23
District 3, Vol. 2	Drawer 53, Box 24
District 4, Vol. 1	Drawer 53, Box 24
District 4, Vol. 2	Drawer 53, Box 25
District 5, Vol. 1	Drawer 53, Box 25
District 5, Vol. 2	Drawer 53, Box 26
District 11, Vol. 1	Drawer 53, Box 27
District 11, Vol. 2	Drawer 53, Box 28
District 12, Vol. 1	Drawer 53, Box 28
District 12, Vol. 2	Drawer 53, Box 29
Districts 13 North, 13 South	Drawer 53, Box 29
District 14, Vols. 1 and 2	Drawer 53, Box 30
District 15	Drawer 53, Box 31

Original Cherokee County, Gold Lottery Map
Section Two

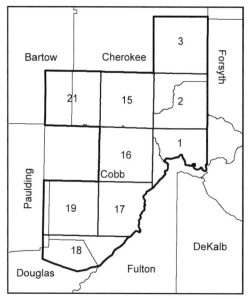

Map 50. Original Cherokee County, Section Two, Gold Lottery.

Original Cherokee County, Gold Lottery Records
Section Two

Plats

Districts	Georgia Archives Microfilm
1–2	Drawer 51, Box 1
3	Drawer 51, Box 2
15–17	Drawer 51, Box 4
18–19	Drawer 51, Box 5
21	Drawer 51, Box 5

Grants

Book	Georgia Archives Microfilm
District 1	Drawer 53, Box 32
District 2, Vols. 1 and 2	Drawer 53, Box 33
District 3, Vols. 1 and 2	Drawer 53, Box 34
District 15, Vols. 1 and 2	Drawer 53, Box 38
District 16, Vols. 1 and 2	Drawer 53, Box 39
District 17, Vols. 1 and 2	Drawer 53, Box 40
District 18	Drawer 53, Box 41
District 19, Vol. 1	Drawer 53, Box 41
District 19, Vol. 2	Drawer 53, Box 42
District 21, Vol. 1	Drawer 53, Box 42
District 21, Vol. 2	Drawer 53, Box 43

Land Lot Size and Orientation, Cherokee Land Lottery

Area: 40 acres
Side: 20 chains or 1,320 feet
Bearing: north

One Mile

Original Cherokee County, Gold Lottery Map
Section Three

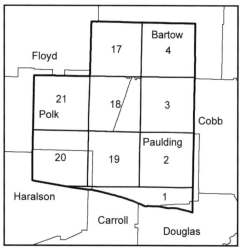

Map 51. Original Cherokee County, Section Three, Gold Lottery.

Original Cherokee County, Gold Lottery Records
Section Three

Plats

Districts	Georgia Archives Microfilm
1–2	Drawer 51, Box 6
3	Drawer 51, Box 7
18–19	Drawer 51, Box 9
20–21	Drawer 51, Box 10

Grants

Book	Georgia Archives Microfilm
District 1	Drawer 53, Box 45
District 2, Vol. 1	Drawer 53, Box 45
District 2, Vol. 2	Drawer 53, Box 46
District 3, Vol. 1	Drawer 53, Box 46
District 3, Vol. 2	Drawer 53, Box 47
District 18, Vol. 1	Drawer 53, Box 52
District 18, Vol. 2	Drawer 53, Box 53
District 19, Vol. 1	Drawer 53, Box 53
District 19, Vol. 2	Drawer 53, Box 54
District 20, Vols. 1 and 2	Drawer 53, Box 54
District 21, Vols. 1 and 2	Drawer 53, Box 55

Land Lot Size and Orientation, Cherokee Gold Lottery

Area: 40 acres
Side: 20 chains or 1,320 feet
Bearing: north

One Mile

Original Cherokee County, Gold Lottery Map
Section Four

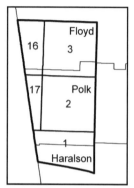

Map 52. Original Cherokee County, Section Four, Gold Lottery.

Original Cherokee County, Gold Lottery Records
Section Four

Plats

Districts	*Georgia Archives Microfilm*
1	Drawer 51, Box 11
2–3	Drawer 51, Box 12
16–17	Drawer 51, Box 14

Grants

Book	*Georgia Archives Microfilm*
District 1	Drawer 53, Box 58
District 2, Vol. 1	Drawer 53, Box 58
District 2, Vol. 2	Drawer 53, Box 59
District 3, Vols. 1 and 2	Drawer 53, Box 59
Districts 16–17	Drawer 54, Box 3

Land Lot Size and Orientation, Cherokee Gold Lottery

Area: 40 acres
Side: 20 chains or 1,320 feet
Bearing: north

One Mile

Qualifications, 1832 Gold Lottery

Requirements (everyone)

U.S. citizen, 3 years

3 years residence in Georgia

Requirements	**Draws**
White male, age 18 or older	One
Widow	One
Family of orphans	One

Additional Draws	
Head of family	One

Excluded

Those whose family did not meet residency requirements, excepting officers of the U.S. Army or Navy

Draft evader

1833 Georgia Fractions Lottery

Treaty	14 March 1835, Washington City (not ratified)
	29 December 1835, New Echota
Law	24 December 1832
Lot Size	Fractions (size varies)
Lot Orientation	0 degrees / 90 degrees
Registration	Within four months after 20 February 1832
Drawing (Land)	6 – 7 December 1833
Drawing (Gold)	9 – 13 December 1833
Reverted Lots	Sold beginning 1 March 1846
First County	Cherokee (see Land and Gold lotteries)
Record	Georgia Archives microfilm, drawer 286, box 49

The 1833 Fractions Lottery distributed fractional lots surveyed in original Cherokee County, as well as lots not drawn in previous lotteries. For maps of land districts, see previous chapters. For an index to fortunate drawers in this lottery, see Robert S. Davis, Jr., *The 1833 Land Lottery of Georgia and Other Missing Names of Winners in the Georgia Land Lotteries*, (Greenville, S.C.: Southern Historical Press, 1991). Grants are recorded in the appropriate district grant books.

Index

Taylor County, 118, 130
Telfair County, 50, 88, 94, 97
Terrell County, 92, 132
Thomas County, 50, 92, 94
Tift County, 94, 120
Towns County, 106, 108, 138
Treaty, 5
Treutlen County, 88
Troup County, 50, 57, 58, 60, 68, 123, 124, 126, 128–29, 130
Turner County, 94, 120
Twiggs County, 50–51, 86, 88, 118

U

Union County, 106, 138, 150
Upson County, 51, 116, 118, 128, 130

W

Walker County, 142, 144
Walton County, 51, 57, 58, 59, 60, 68, 86, 91, 100–101, 102, 112
Ware County, 51, 82, 97
Warren County, 51
Washington County, 51, 80, 88
Wayne County, 51, 57, 58, 68, 77, 82–83, 97
Webster County, 132
Wheeler County, 88
White County, 104, 106, 108, 138
Whitfield County, 142
Wilcox County, 88, 94, 120
Wilkes County, 33, 51–52
Wilkinson County, 52, 57, 58, 59, 68, 77, 78, 80–81, 85, 88–90
Worth County, 92, 94, 120, 132